J.C. Vintner

Ancient World Mysteries

by

J. C. Vintner

The journey and experience.

This publication includes encounters, interpretations, and beliefs prompting the publication of the Ancient Earth Mysteries series. With this commentary, contents include the complete AEM series of books, namely Ancient Earth Mysteries, Mysteries of the Universe, and Legendary Cryptids.

ANCIENT WORLD MYSTERIES

Table of Contents

J.C. Vintner

Thought is one of the most
powerful gifts given to mankind.

Introduction

Confronting inner demons is by no means an easy adventure in any stretch of the imagination. Facing personal turmoil is terrifying, overwhelming, and down right spooky. Yet by doing so, doorways open to the mind and soul, which without doubt demonstrate the true potential of an individual encased by our universal self. The experience liberates an inner cosmic child who then awakens to realize no longer are they an infant born to the universe, but instead an intricate part of its grand design.

When this awakening happened to me, it was absolutely confusing at first, and for a good while I didn't understand what was happening. A friend of mine even told me when I arrived back home after the event, "You don't know what's going on, do you?" The comment and the atmosphere surrounding it still resonates to this day. At the time, in my own odd realm of clarity, everything made sense as it unfolded; I eventually felt privileged to be part of whatever it this awakening event was, and eager to learn my place. To close friends though, I must have appeared dazed and out of it for days, because it changed who I am as a person and taught me where I belong.

During the more clairvoyant moments I can recall an overwhelming sense of acceptance, as being accompanied by greater forces, ready to witness my challenge. They anticipated my ability to face life in the darkest of avenues, to move on, adapt, and overcome. Granted, this experience did not come without a price, a toll the mind pays on a daily basis to sit with the creators but once in a lifetime. In the previous statement this condition may sound as more of a burden than a blessing, but I assure you on several levels do I feel fortunate for the opportunity.

A short series of events managed to change everything I know about existence as individuals to a more universal realization. The first realization, is in fact, that we really are not individuals, but instead a part of a vast collective composed of precious energy. Contemplations later in life would soon mate this realization to a fundamental concept, conservation of energy. The first law of thermodynamics tells us energy may change forms from one state to another, but it may not be created or destroyed. Given this, and the fact we are all beings of energy, it is appropriately fitting we, as energy, may only change forms from one state to another, and not be created, nor destroyed.

Undoubtedly this is a profound statement about life, and who we truly are in the bigger picture. I have spent time throughout my life thinking and trying to understand what exactly this means, as I know in a literal sense my biological form on Earth is meant to one day pass. The energy which brings me life, though, it must pass on according simply to thermodynamics. To some this might be reincarnation or an afterlife, and to others a transcendence into heaven, hell, or purgatory. One of the greatest, most mysterious questions ever asked by any civilization, past or present, seeks to answer where energy of the mind and soul venture to the moment our physical flesh expires from Earth.

Truth and purity coalesce in our everyday existence, which helps shape realization to know there are indeed more complex dimensional levels in the universe beyond those which we are privileged to understand. This residual part, in a number of ways, is meant to differentiate between past truths and events responsible for creating who we are. The next realization. Personal trials of the past are no more important than anyone else's, as those trials are respective, individual links connecting each of us to the grand design.

Imagine this similarly to the very creation overwhelming the modern world at this moment, the Internet. Often the world wide web is simply described as a network of computers connected together to share information and communicate. From another perspective, though, the Internet manages to easily connect people's minds together with a gigantic network of recursive technologies. Perhaps this is the beginning of a realized global mind and a lead-in to the eventually connectivity with the universal mind.

Are we the architects of this significant transformation in human existence? Years of soul-searching, accompanied by the occasional extreme situation, brought further realizations and epiphanies. I stimulated a unique level of thinking in isolation with ritualistic practices designed to invoke the most purely honest, sincere reflections upon my very soul. "Be true to yourself, right?"

I took the plunge, opening one of the darkest doors in my mind, and I can tell you honestly, the outcome was not at all by intention. This was at the start, of a short series of events which managed to change everything I know about existence. Prior to the events I didn't have too much interest in otherworldly beings, ghosts, mysterious places, megalithic structures, other dimensions, aliens, or cryptids. With newfound knowledge, I'm positively able to look back at these moments and conclude the experience itself is very similar to ancient adulthood rituals.

My mind faced a prolonged period of darkness in order to confront my demons, and from this I began to learn who I really am. Early childhood memories are vague at best guess, so it's difficult to understand events years prior to the life changing experience. What I can remember feels necessary to be told, to help build a better idea of who I am, and to help others. As I trace thoughts backwards, certain events stick out. To me, those memories are photographically vivid, clear and sharp as a bright as if they happened only yesterday. I sometimes hold their replays as a type of reasoning to my existence, that maybe I am able to view those thoughts fluidly for a more profound reason. One of these events happened on an average day in third grade, while learning to write cursive, well before a personal conscious awakening.

A religious school I attended at a very young age disciplined their students with a more strict approach to Biblical teachings. It was natural for me at that time, to hold a pencil with my left hand, but unfortunately this was least desirable to the cursive class instructor. "Writing with your left hand is a sign of the devil!" Yes, literally she told me this. At this age, I had no clue what it meant, nor did I understand the connection she made. In fact, it's difficult to recall a Sunday school lesson telling kids which hand they should write with.

After this, and not directly related, I noticed family appearances at Catholic masses gradually receded until the point of not going at all. There were other life factors beyond my knowledge involved in the family's decision. Eventually we switched to a Baptist church, a night and day difference compared to Catholic services in my mind. Instead of mourning sins, and teachings to repent our very existence, the Baptist church asked us to stand and praise.

In these moments I felt more aware of life's existence, awakening inside, opening my mind to a more receptive state. For a period in the span of three years our family said goodbye to great Oma on my dad's side, Oma, Opa, an uncle, and an aunt. The timing, surreal, for any family to have to go through. Seeing my relatives pass on brought about questions of life, wanting to know where they have gone, and wondering if I will see them again.

Looking back at family losses is painful at times, but in some ways there is a comfortable feeling to believe their energy has moved on to another part of existence, perhaps to a place weren't not meant to physically see while on

Earth. It was during this time, that I started researching life's mysteries. Reading books in university libraries, scanning microfiche at town libraries, looking for relevant documentation on-line, and delving into historical archives.

After some research, the lessons taught in Sunday school took on an whole new perspective. Answers slowly revealed themselves in curious ways, helping to develop my own understanding of existence. I found comfort knowing we all must live for a purpose, even if we're not immediately aware of that purpose, and events of my childhood are somehow a part of it. The reason to live may not be one we know or understand, or something we are comfortable dealing with, but eventually we all discover what this purpose is. For many years I thought, maybe perhaps, that when someone discovers the true meaning of life on Earth, they pass on before having the ability to tell anyone the secret.

Another possible explanation is something I have contemplated time and time again, an interesting concept my wife brings up whenever we get on the subject. She theorizes that what if perhaps, in some way, we decide destiny before birth, as goals or lessons to learn during our time on Earth before moving on. To add to this, a guardian of sorts watches over and helps us to realize our goals. The key is, however, that we are not consciously aware of the lessons and goals we decided for ourselves. Those details, and the details of other realms, exist only depending on relative location.

One intriguing research paper from my studies talks about ancient history with respect to the many possible ways content of the Bible can be portrayed, that often verses may be taken out of context in order to facilitate a specific message at a church service. The messenger's objective. A tactic sometimes used by false prophets to gain power over people using the words of scripture. Although controversial, it suggested ways ministers may intentionally choose passages from the book to justify their own preaching even if those passages didn't fit the true message or accepted belief.

Incidentally, congregations may only hear a part of the story offered as a solution to life's current moment. Only one phrase of the whole. It becomes the listener's responsibility to decide how the message fits either within Biblical context, or in their own life, as the message may not be entirely complete. The level of perception is one way in which control over others may be gained, by leaving a strategical open-ended statement to be solved with an almighty answer.

Perhaps, thought, it could be a condition of the human psyche. If one desirably looks for a pattern, they are more likely to find it, and more likely to have their brain adapt a pattern which might not otherwise be known. From this, I sought to discover what the Bible is really saying, despite many old, mixed-English translations, alternate language texts, and ancient stone-carved scripts. Then, more importantly, I sought to discover why Biblical verses hold an immensely significant value to a large number of people around the world.

Wording of ancient Biblical texts is certainly unique, even after thousands of years of translations. Books of several prophets emphasize distinct characteristics and life's values in relation to a higher power, to whom we are mere mortals in comparison and unworthy. Beyond this, some stories speak of face-to-face (and even telepathic) interactions with angelic beings who appear to have human-like qualities by way of description.

Humans with wings? If taken literally, it's incredible to think our ancestors were privileged to speak with and see those who created life on Earth, and their messengers, isn't it? Except this begs for an answer to a largely important question. Why would life's creators and messengers, of the heavens, Earth, and life upon it, make direct contact with our ancestors, and not with mankind in the present day at the same level of blatancy as described in the Bible? Over two thousand years, or potentially more, have passed.

What if, perhaps, scriptures of the world's religions truly date back to thousands of years ago before written language. To an ancient time when knowledge bestowed upon man from the heavens had only word of mouth and pictographs to carry messages throughout generations. One theory suggests ancient gods, deities, and messengers have been trying to intentionally contact us all along. The case may be that we're simply just unreceptive to the type of message, or unable to understand we're being contacted at all.

Some believe the message is here now, and we're not taking it seriously. Perhaps instead, it's the advent of scientific reasoning through a significant mathematical understanding, which enables us to unknowingly communicate with life's creators. Or perhaps, mankind's perception of reality is a strange misconception, one changing ever so dynamically over time, in accordance with a morphing connectivity in a global mind.

In the Shadows
(Rite of Passage)

Loss of close family at an early age was the blessing in disguise then inspiring me to ask more questions than ever before, questions which in time would lead to an unforgettable series of events responsible for changing my life forever. What happened next shook the foundation of reality, a glimpse into the future, custom tailored to my cosmic place in connection with the universal mind. I physically walked through shadows of darkness for many hours to develop strong psychic bridges. They provided specific details of future events pertaining to my future life. When the experience took place, it was not understood the visions were really premonitions. Amidst the moment of clairvoyance I was unaware of reality, floating in uncontrollable moments like a waking dream beyond all capability.

In the short period before setting out on this journey, my research lead to exploring realms of chaotic theory and constant string theorem. These fresh ideas may or may not have influenced the outcome directly, but those principals helped identify where we fit as humans. I can recall how the state was entered, fine details of the visions, and how the experience changed my conscious being. The spiritual connection faded eventually, and achieving clairvoyance for the first time in my life was completely unintentional.

It begins with a series of events filled with commotion in a house brought about by an urgent matter. A group of friends asked me to take part in a trip, and I really wasn't sure if it was the wisest of ideas at that point in time. In fact, I really did not want to go, but the reluctance was soon to pass. The group met up with two people from overseas who tagged along. One was a man of the cross, and the other, a mysterious dark-eyed woman, both who were adamant the lot of us explore a few large hostels in the area. Nervous thoughts toiled, over an opportunity to discover an area with a controversial reputation, tucked away far from the mainstream.

Thirteen of us set out on a beautiful day with the sun shining bright, a deep blue sky as far as we could see and light puffy clouds dotting the distance. The gorgeous weather gave a feeling as though this trip was meant to happen. Unknown to me at the time, would this beauty turn into a much darker, sinister existence later that night. We arrived about an hour before dusk, parked in a huge lot, and found ourselves in a strange seedy place after a half an hour's walk. The secret community bustled like an unkempt bowel of the city. Everywhere we looked, wandering eyes of people glanced back, and behind those people were more eyes. Shifty, shady eyes moving every which way. Through doors, down winding paths shrouded in trees, up flights of stairs, flowing from room to room in the shelter areas. There were beds and bunks at every turn; Many were occupied by one or two people sleeping in clothes, using backpacks as pillows. Walls and room dividers partially existed, appropriately complementing any notion of privacy or personal space.

In the sea of people and eyes, I became separated from the group on several occasions, but each time this happened, we eventually found each other again. Most of us could not afford mobile phones, but we had a plan to meet at a certain checkpoint every so often. The next time I was separated from the group, nobody could be found at the checkpoint. I held tight for a while, waiting, and eventually falling half-asleep on one of the empty bunk mattresses. Early the next morning I woke up to the sun rise beaming into my eyes. The group, still nowhere to be found.

I walked around the immediate vicinity, looking to see if maybe our group crashed nearby. With no luck there, I traced my steps from the previous night, thinking maybe I'd be able to find at least one person from the group, but that too turned no results. So it was back to the parking lot only to find the car was gone too. Now worries took over as I realized the group either took off without me, or all three cars were stolen. Left in a strange place ten hours from home with no ride and very little money. It was noon by the time I realized just how bad the situation became.

The general idea now, to find some public transportation such as a taxi, train, or bus station to make it home. It sounded simple enough then, in my mind, but the truth of the matter brings me to life realization number three; Becoming lost is a true test to one's perseverance and ambition. Being a fair distance from main street traffic, and having an elevated level of anxiety, I decided to continue walking.

Three hours, three coffees, a sub, and a mind full of thoughts later. Lovely, nourishing sustenance. Now I finally start seeing taxis to hail, but with a limited cash supply, I had to continue walking. Going from shop to shop, asking for directions to the nearest bus or train depot. The language barrier made it difficult to understand what anyone was saying. My lack of knowledge of the city streets along with thick accents turned the situation into a dire one. I've gone over the edge of a rabbit hole. At first it was captivating exploring the city, thinking it would be easy to find my way, but it all changed that night when darkness fell. Hours passed by and I soon found myself walking through dark alleys and down deserted dark city streets.

No sleep and continuous walking. I recited Psalms 23 to while venturing through some of the darker areas. No longer looking focusing on a train station or a bus station. I was lost and afraid. This became my rite of passage into adulthood. Hours of walking and thinking put my body and mind into another state of being. Eventually I felt like I couldn't possibly take another step. With daylight breaking I stopped to rest on the upward slope of hill in a nearby park. I laid back and looked toward the sky, taking a few thoughts to admire its beauty and potentially distract my mind from the stress it's under. Transportation home still seemed too far away.

At this point I gave thanks for getting through the night safely and felt my mind slipping away into a peaceful consciousness. I still didn't feel safe enough to sleep, and did my best not to close my eyes. After some time looking at the sky, visions appeared as if entering some sort of trance-like state. Two mysterious figures were talking to each other in an unknown language, in atmosphere resembling otherworldly isolation from Earth. We were the only entities in a white, mist-filled auditorium. Vocals met my ears in soft, gentle, echoing whispers, and psychedelic visuals played out across the sky in a waking dream. Together, the two beings told several stories using whispers and visualizations about people and events which were difficult to recognize at first.

Oddly, in this moment, I could not understand the spoken language but somehow it translated to English in my mind.

One of the visions described an hierarchy of knowledge with a game similar to chess. The difference, though, is this black and white checkered board was so infinitely huge that an end could not be seen over any horizon. Pieces on the board were not carved figures representing royal armies, but instead real people on a path of life. The two celestial figures demonstrated their ability to move human game pieces to meet each other and face predetermined life challenges. Unlike chess, though, human pieces on the board did not proceed to overtake tiles in triumph. They joined together by streams of light for each connection, much like descriptions of constant string theorem.

Another vision portrayed a blonde woman directing her two children out of harm's way, looking mildly frantic yet in complete control of the situation. A pleasant fragrance filled the air for a few moments accompanied by a strong uplifting feeling. During this moment, the visions began to fade with one final whisper saying "Once a glimpse is seen, it may not be unseen." The mist-filled auditorium then lowered as a floating veil, and the moment it came in contact with my body, everything disappeared. Clouds went back to rolling in the distance, and the sky, back to its blue hue. Fragrance in the air became infused with cut grass, and those gentle echoing whispers turned into birds chirping. Across the park, in the haze of the city, a train depot sign suddenly caught my attention.

J.C. Vintner

Ancient Earth Mysteries

In life, we are given signs to help lead us on our way through the best and worst of times. We can always forgive ourselves for our mistakes, but it's learning from them which helps us grow. I have found myself in several situations throughout life that have been both difficult and stressful, but it is hope and belief in something beyond who we are in the physical realm that keeps me looking for more answers. I have felt more attuned to the cosmos after becoming lost in a major city, walking around for two days straight drinking coffee, and having a truly life changing spiritual pilgrimage. It may sound crazy and unfortunate to some, to perceive what happened in my past the way I do, but in the very least it opened my eyes to a much larger existence even if I am but a pawn in its game of chess.

One of the my first theoretical questions of our existence and events in the Bible comes from the book of Genesis, in the Garden of Eden, and a flaming sword turning in every which way to keep Adam away from the Tree of Life. For some reason after reading these passages, I wondered if the flaming sword might be a literal identification, perhaps say for that of a plant like the rosette Bromeliad Vriesea splendens, also known today as a Flaming Sword plant. This particular plant is naturally found in Venezuela and Suriname, far from the Biblical cradle of life's location today.

A correlation here comes from the Book of Exodus and the burning bush. Some believe Moses must have been hallucinating to claim he witnessed both a bush on fire without being consumed and the ghostly apparition of god inside it. There is actually a bush which catches on fire in hot weather, known as the Dictamnus albus, and certain varieties are found in the Mediterranean area. Could this be the bush Moses speaks of? Is it possible god presented himself through the heat distortion effect emitted from the burning bush? If Moses recorded events based truly on a real plant, then what about the Flaming Sword, and the Tree of Life for that matter?

We know Dictamnus can be found roughly in the same area where Moses claimed to see god, There are at least two theoretically possible ways the Flaming Sword native to Venezuela could be placed partway around the world into the Biblical cradle. One, trading between South American cultures and perhaps Egyptians. Remnants of psychoactive substances along with plants and artifacts native to South America have been discovered in Egyptian tombs.

Evidence loosely creates a link between the two distant continents though hasn't provided solid proof. The idea is not far off Columbus introducing another Bromeliad species, the pineapple, to Spain around 500 years ago.

The second theory suggests something fairly startling with a rather large time factor involved. Around 237 million years ago in the Early Triassic, Venezuela and Suriname were located right on the edge of Africa as Earth's landmass clumped together as Pangea. If a similar Flaming Sword variety of Bromeliad existed at this time, and spanned into northern Africa, could it be what Genesis talked of in Eden?

References to the Burning bush, Flaming Sword, and Tree of Life are a few of many mysteries in our ancient past. All around the world we find countless mysterious treasures, strange artifacts, and megalithic structures which were once the everyday pride of our ancient ancestors. Time may have buried many objects along with their secrets. Modern archeology and the persistence of many inquisitive individuals is helping to uncover the truth of our past. Science has only scratched the surface of a vast amount of information locked in time. Only a small fraction of artifacts estimated to exist have been discovered. There is an aching thirst to find out more about our history with every clue. Large gaps of missing items, fragmented remains and partial information makes the process of rediscovering our human roots much like digging through a very long and dark rabbit hole. How far does it go? Is there a light in sight, at all?

One answer has eluded mankind since the dawn of existence. One definitive answer satisfying all pent up curiosities thousands and thousands of years in the making. The next most amazing concept since the discovery of fire. So what is it? Who are we? Why is life the way it is? These questions have motivated people as far back as historical records go. It makes sense that many of questions similar to these were asked verbally before the dawn of written language. The very first Egyptian Hieroglyph depicts a wine press. Surely the Egyptians practiced and perfected the art of wine making for a longer period of time than our historical record indicates.

Information found in this book is based on tangible evidence of existing places and artifacts obtained from long hours of research. Certain ideas cover highly controversial and deeply speculated topics from rudimentary perspectives. The goal of this concept is to provide ample opportunity for deciphering meaning in both introspective and broad realms. Discovering a single answer to why humans exist is not an easy task considering the insurmountable amount of variables. As much as mankind has learned over the past thousands of years, it is still believed by some that life on Earth remains in a period of infancy.

In the past, our ancient ancestors lived in tight knit social communities where many of their activities were contingent on social interactions like hunting, gathering, and cooking. We know before modern technologies, food and spirituality were primary focal points for everyday life according to mainstream sciences. Each day, dedicated researchers bring new evidence to light which continuously dates cultures to be older and alters the perspective of our past. For a while science believed the oldest civilization was a mere 5,000 years, consistent with quite a few cultural beliefs. Then artifacts and settlements were found, pushing the date back 10-12,000 years. Theorists now estimate civil cultures as old as 35-40,000 years based on a recent climate discovery purposing an ancient migration route through the North American ice sheet. Meanwhile, molecular and fossil science states that modern humans originated in Africa some 100 to 200 thousand years ago.

There is one absolutely unquestionable and easily identifiable transcendence from ancient culture to ancient culture. Our past ancestors uniformly believed in something greater than their own existence. Many today still exhibit the same or a very similar principal belief. Changes in technology put these beliefs to the test, essentially forcing an adjustment in personal values.

Reoccurring fears of an apocalypse or doomsday event have cycled throughout the ages. Prophecy is not a modern practice. The reality of modern technology, and its rate of acceleration, may very well be the top contributing factors to End of the World theories becoming more wide-spread. Couple technology with the vast amount of information we've learned about our past. As a species we are progressing.

Modern technology truly is unbelievably impressive and the leaps mankind made in the last two hundred years is a monumental testament to our deep-rooted perseverance. By in part, new technology can also be blinding in the way we perceive our past. It's easy to look at modern technology and simply say the past is primitive by comparison. The picture is slowly revealing itself and proving our ancestors were not nearly as primitive as once thought. In fact, so much evidence has been uncovered about our ancestors. Some modern theorists believe the only possible explanation is there must be an outside influence or even physical help from other worldly beings.

We have only scratched the surface of an unfathomable time-line. Science can theoretically trace particle existence to a time long ago when matter was concentrated to a very small, dense point in the sky. Given the scope and size of the Universe according to physics it seems selfish to think Earth bares the only living byproducts of such a grand scale explosion. Finite odds alone tell us there is no conceivable way only one living planet would result from an infinite number of possibilities.

Even-though we have not yet discovered a means of physically traversing the Universe quickly and safely doesn't mean that it's not attainable. Spirituality and cross-cultural religious beliefs share common elements with theoretical sciences in the pursuit of truth. Both science and religion acknowledge the existence of something greater than ourselves although exactly what the something is differs by perspectives.

Intriguing and complex archaeological sites found around the world paint a picture; One not of primitive mindset but one of increasing fascination of the heavens and stars above. Many structures have astrological translations and concepts with deep cosmological influences. According to carbon dating and scientific evidence, these structures were commonly built at a time when the night sky was darker. Current accepted beliefs claim that electricity was not harnessed or used in any form during the period.

Modern theories state our ancestors were forced to navigate by the stars and sun alone. Old farmer's almanac woodcuts and structures were aligned by the night sky, marking the solstices for times to plant and harvest. Prominent celestial events witnessed were recorded, eventually becoming additional markers for significant spiritual points of contact.

Mankind has an insatiable appetite for knowledge especially when it involves where we came from and who we really are. It is not unreasonable by any means for humanity to ensure anything we know about our past is as accurate as possible. As a guide to our ancient past it is the intention to provide a collective of research toned to a neutral point. We trust this information will be utilized for greater purpose.

Ancient Astronauts

Digging deep into history to the beginning of written record, and verbal legend, uncovers a massive resource of astonishing knowledge. Our ancestors depict their daily lives and the world in vivid detail. Evidence suggests ancient civilizations were much more technologically advanced than ever imagined. Records suggesting our ancestors once communicated with beings from the sky are continuously being discovered.

Stories and legends across multiple ancient cultures seem to point toward similar concepts even in scenarios where those cultures are believed to have never interacted with each other. One critical reoccurring theme spanning ancient civilizations refers to beings visiting Earth from the skies above. Many cultures have carvings, glyphs, and relics which demonstrate with modern interpretation how they might have been interacting with astronauts of some kind, alien to planet Earth. Ancient astronaut relics portray modern space suits and diving outfits as well as many, what we currently know as, modern technologies. To some, these historical accounts, alien relics, and ancient ruins provide some indication of technologies beyond those of current capability.

Sumerian Anunnaki

Appropriately fitting we begin with one of the oldest known cultures with written language. Cuneiform script written on clay tablets Ancient Sumerian texts define the Anunnaki as "those who from heaven to Earth came" described as those who descended from the heavens. Certain contexts attribute the Anunnaki as the fallen angels.

By comparative religions, it's believed the book of Genesis, estimated date of 600 BCE, was extracted from the Sumerian Epic of Creation, with an estimated ~6000-8500 BCE date of creation. Archeology can actually place the Sumerian Epic creation only by a small tablet fragment which dates by the script to 2150 BCE, much later than theorized estimates. Sumerian records are filled with great details and depictions demonstrating the Anunnaki as the watchers which is also evident in further Biblical texts by Daniel and Jubilees.

Abraham's father Terah once served the fallen angels, or the sons of the gods and goddesses, according to Psalms, with reference to the Nephilim. Sharing part of the Babylonian creation myth as the children of Anu and Ki, the Anunnaki are also associated with the stories of the 12th planet (Planet X theory), and its return to

Earth over a long elliptical orbit. As the Sumerian portray the Anunnaki as watchers, they also touch upon further controversial concepts.

According to Sumerian accounts, Anunnaki were the gods and goddesses who met occasionally to indirectly determine the fate of mankind if by no fault of their own. Sumerian believed their society was a slave race serving the efforts of the Anunnaki who were here on Earth to mine gold to repair their home planet's atmosphere. Theorists state, based on these Sumerian texts, the possibility existing in which the Anunnaki actually took an Earth species and gifted just enough knowledge to complete the mining operation without troubles. Mega ancient gold mines were discovered in South America, lending merit to the idea however a solidified link has not been found.

In the Enuma Elish (Epic of Creation) one may also find several references to dragons and half-man half-beast creations. Variations of these beasts play an important role in cultural beliefs of nearly every ancient civilization known to history:

"She set up vipers and dragons, and the monster Lahamu,
And hurricanes, and raging hounds, and scorpion-men,
And mighty tempests, and fish-men, and rams;"

Dogon Tribe

Currently located in Mali West Africa is a tribe known to have a rich astronomically influenced history dating back to around 3200 BC. To some theorists the Dogon are believed to have descended from ancient Egyptians and possessed extraterrestrial knowledge of the stars. Deeply rooted traditions of the Dogon speak about Nommos, who visited from a companion star to Sirius. The Nommos are amphibious beings who have also appear in numerous related myths found in Babylonian, Acadia, and Sumerian cultures.

Sirius' companion star has a 50 year elliptical orbit and is not visible to the naked eye. Modern astronomers did not know the companion star existed until the Dogon myth was discovered. They tell us the Nommos shared knowledge of Sirius with them and left behind several artifacts. One artifact depicting the Sirius constellation carbon dates to 400 years ago, a little over 230 years before astronomers first suspected the existence of a companion star.

Every 60 years the Dogon celebrate the cycle of Sirius A and B which raises further questions considering Sirius B's 50 year cycle. Dogon legend mentions a 3rd star in the system, which would be called Sirius C if found by modern telescopes. Nommos are believed to inhabit a planet orbiting Sirius C though mainstream science does not consider the Sirius constellation to be a prime candidate for life. Research in 1995 concluded based on observations of motions in the Sirius system, a red dwarf star about $1/20^{th}$ the mass of Sirius B exists.

Hopi Indians

"The Peaceful People" live in northeast Arizona to this present day. Hopi Indians are considered as descendants from cultures to the north, east and south. One of their ancestors is the Anasazi, who directly relate to the Aztec culture. Although many civilizations maintain creation beliefs rooted with gods descending from the sky, the Hopi believe their ancestors ascended from the Earth.

One Hopi legend specifically referrers to the Ant People who inhabit the heart of the Earth. Depictions of Ant People strongly resemble modern day gray alien sighting reports. The Hopi believe at the end of the current cycle of time, star people and star knowledge will return. Blue Kachina, when star people went to the heart of the Earth to be protected during apocalyptic destruction of the last cycle of time.

Legend of the Blue Kachina coincides with Mayan prophecy, suggesting an interconnection between Hopi beliefs and those of the Ancient Mayans. Further Hopi prophecies relate to similar creation stories found throughout different cultures. The tribe believes five stone tablets existed at the time of creation. One kept by the creator, two given to the Hopi themselves, and two given to brothers in history to be brought together when the world reunites in peace.

Renaissance Art

Intriguing elements exist in several paintings by artists from the Renaissance period up until the French Revolution. Some of the paintings were fully explained and proved not to have any extraterrestrial influence according to art historian experts in the field. Certain elements found in the paintings catch the eyes of Ancient Alien theorists. The Cardinal hat is sometimes mistaken as a UFO. An object which resembles a modern satellite is considered a depiction of the universe creation sphere. Other mistaken elements sometimes include a dove, which is representative of the Holy Spirit, and light rays or speculated to be associated with the disc shaped objects.

As true art should be, interpretation relies solely on the subjected audience. Personal beliefs, values, and impressions may skew artwork meaning far from the artist's intended message. The following artworks are referred to by Ancient Astronaut theorists to have significant value to the overall theory, which encompasses a very large array of disciplines and is not stringent upon the content of any one specific art piece.

Baptism of Christ

Aert De Gelder 1710 BCE. A very intriguing art piece in a series from De Gelder, this one displays the Baptism of Christ and presents quite a few questions regarding composition. In the 1,700's Aert studied under Rembrandt. He was believed to be Rembrandt's brightest student and most avid follower. Rembrandt's influence seems to be the only solid theory as to why De Gelder painted original elements into his works do not jive with other artists during the period.

Aert's Baptism of Christ displays a circular formation in the sky with several rays of light shining upon Jesus. The circle is not composed of a series of cherubs, nor is the dove or Holy Spirit traditionally portrayed. Although the composition doesn't seem to follow common traditions depicted by other artists during the same period, it does not necessarily mean Aert's message isn't one in the same.

Disputa of the Eucharist

Bonaventura Salimbeni 1600 BCE. This painting is representative of a creation sphere meant to depict the universe as a whole with the Holy Trinity. Certain intriguing aspects have not been answered. Jesus and the Father are holding wands which gives the impression of Sputnik, though we know this to be highly unlikely.

Another interesting section of the painting is where Jesus and the Father are pointing and why. The grip on the wands in a penmanship-like fashion gives the impression of precision as markings found throughout the artwork. Perhaps Salimbeni was trying to draw attention to his finely detailed masterpiece.

Madonna with Saint Giovannino

Domenico Ghirlandaio. A puzzling object found in the top right corner of this painting has the striking resemblance of a modern UFO but the mystery deepens when a man and his dog looking upward at a strange object. They are found just along the shoreline, directly to the right of the Madonna's left shoulder. It is quite possible this subtle touch by Ghirlandaio was designed to further emphasize the presence of the Holy Spirit during the sacred conversation.

Annunciation with Saint Emidius

Carlo Crivelli 1486. A ray of light emanating from a disc shaped cloud formation in the sky, directed through an opening in a building to the Dove and Mother Mary. The area of interest isn't necessarily the circular cloud disc of cherubs in the sky or the beam of light which may seem odd. Common accouterments found in an alchemist's study where Mother Mary is located is what raises questioning.

The painting's period is during a time when Alchemy was viewed as deceptive practice and banned from for 200 years by Pope John XX II, King Charles V, King Henry IV, King Henry VI, and both cities of Venice and Nuremberg. Pope Sixtus IV granted the town of Ascoli a degree of self-government and this painting was the altarpiece for the church of SS Annunziata. Does this depict Mother Mary embracing the liberty of Ascoli by visiting the local Alchemist?

Visoki Decani Monastery

1350. Located in the Serbian province of Kosovo, the beautiful Visoki Decani Monastery is a well decorated home to several period relics of saints, including the entire preserved body of St. King Stefan of Decani. Among many frescoes, one stands alone in describing the crucifixion of Christ. In each top corner is what appears to be a flying craft with a human figure inside.

Ume No Chiri – Dust of Apricot

An 1803 book titled Ume No Chiri describes a foreign ship and crew witnessed at Hratonohama in Hitachi No Kuni Japan. The mysterious craft is described to be built from iron and red sandalwood, with glass-crystal fit windows. Strange picture glyphs from an unknown language decorate the interior. The encounter proceeds to describe a young woman leaving the ship while holding a mysterious wooden box.

Annales Laurissenses

776. Several scholars claim the two Laurissenses images circulating the Internet, supposedly extracted from an Annales manuscript to be faked. They can't explain the actual text documented at the time. In Maiores MGH SRG 6 on page 44 there is a passage which describes watchmen witnessing two large, reddish-colored flaming shields moving above the church the very moment the Saxons were preparing to attack the Christians, who reoccupied the castle once again. The script specifically refers to the large flaming shields as the manifestation of God directly above the church.

Miracle of the Snow

Masolino Da Panicale 1432. Painted to honor the foundation of Santa Maria Maggiore, the Miracle of the Snow is based on a legend from the year 352. Pope Liberius and Giovanni had a dream of Mother Mary asking to have a church built on one of the seven hills of Rome. She told them it would snow in the location where the church is to be constructed. According to the legend, it snowed in an exact square where claimed and the first church in honor of Mother Mary was built in place. The Miracle of the Snow legend is also linked to a reported event in 1954 over Florence Italy, when several flying discs left a cotton-like discharge as they flew by. The shape of the clouds in Panicale's painting are not normal cloud shapes commonly found in other paintings during the same period, resulting in speculation to the true meaning.

Dharamsala Temple

According to repeated sources found on the Internet, there are paintings displaying UFOs in the Dharamsala Temple, site of the Dalai Lama's living quarters. In traditional Tibetan art, such as the image of 1000 Buddhas, it is very evident such an interpretation may be perceived from the artwork. Rather than for self-expression, Tibetan art is a tool for enlightenment with emphasis placed on the sacred process, and often with Tantric qualities instead of purely aesthetic properties. Many painted deities appear in a meditative sitting position. Sometimes they're depicted well above the ground level to project the deity as floating in the sky. The detail surrounding the seat and deity demonstrates possible propulsion systems leading theorists to believe the paintings incorporate ancient alien aircraft.

Beyond the artwork are many stories and legends passed down which speak of gods who fought battles in the sky and flying objects known as Vimanas. Historical accounts spanning multiple cultures correlate and corroborate stories of ancient flying aircraft. A long record of historical accounts embrace these legends suggesting there might be a connection between written Vimana legends and the deity imagery found throughout related Tibetan artwork. Perhaps meditation is necessary to effectively control the aircraft. It could be possible that more emphasis was placed on the imagery of the deity simply because they were of flesh and blood. However the artwork is looked upon, uncertainties in interpretation raise questions and inspire us to think there may be something further.

Nuremberg 1561

In 1561, Hans Glaser documented a strange event on a woodcut for the Nuremberg Gazette. Described as hundreds of crosses, globes and tubes fighting each other above the city. Some of the objects were reported to disappear into the sun, and others into a thick cloud of smoke after crashing into the ground. Many citizens witnessed the entire spectacle along with the appearance of a large black, spear-like object after the battle. According to the accounts, not only did people of the 16th century witness what seems to be a UFO battle, they were also able to distinctly tell which side was winning.

Along with the occurrence in Nuremberg, five years later in 1566, citizens of Basel Switzerland witnessed a similar spectacle involving several black orbs engaged in battle filling the sky above. The people of Basel also recorded the event in their city gazette with a woodcut that cannot be traced to a known artist. Accounts claim the black orbs would sometimes turn red and fiery before fading to nothing.

Dropa Stones

Inside a cave found in the Himalayan mountains, a professor of archeology and his students stumbled upon a very large cache of 12,000 year old stone discs and several 4 foot tall skeletons. Each stone disc is about one foot wide and features two fine grooves inscribed which spiral from the edge to the disc's ¾" center hole. In the cave where the Dropa Stones were found, the walls were carved with depictions of the sun, moon, and stars, along with several small dots connecting the Earth to the sky.

The 716 stone discs found are not quite like the Phaistos Disc of Greece, though they are also finely decorated with a series of glyphs. Dropa glyphs on the stones are so small that a magnifying glass is required to read them and several have succumbed to erosion over the years. Due to both of these factors, and the language itself, a definitive translation is still not available. Controversy over non-glyph discs and researchers attempting to translate the contents has lead skepticism willing to dismiss any and all credible evidence along with related theories. It would be very difficult to decipher a language with an unknown source or without any foundation based on known human languages. Until links are found, literally connecting the dots of the Dropa Stones, the translations and true answers remain a mystery.

Quimbaya

According to mainstream archeology, pre-columbian Quimbaya culture is believed to be the inhabitants of South America from 300 to 1550 CE. Quimbaya are best known for their precise gold and metalwork. The majority of gold pieces discovered are made from a tumbaga alloy with 30% copper, very similar to those accounts mentioned by Plato in his dialogs about the lost city of Atlantis. The intricate gold works include several types of insects.

Two pieces distinctly stand out to be aerodynamic in nature and do not resemble any other known insect with the same details and characteristics. The pieces look very much like the designs of modern airplanes and incorporate a number of features essentially proving the

Quimbaya knew and understood the principals of flight. Scale replicas of the golden flier were built five times larger and tested precisely. Results from the tests showed these airplane shaped devices were capable of flight and flew perfectly without any modifications using modern techniques.

Wondjina

Ancient Australian Aboriginal mythology suggests the rain and cloud spirits would descend from the sky to paint Wandjina figures on cave walls. Aboriginal culture mandates the paints to be refreshed on a regular basis by the current oldest living descendant. The process is believed to date back to the original prehistoric Aborigines. Wondjina cave paintings of rain and cloud spirits resemble modern ghost and alien depictions. The Wondjina believe dream-time is also cosmological time and the principal order of all things to exist in the universe. Interpretations of the paintings claim the figures do not contain mouths otherwise it would continue to rain without relief.

It's also interesting to note a few of the Wondjina drawings demonstrate ascension, or an upward movement toward the heavens. Although interpretation tells us Wandjina represent rain spirits, there seems to be much more to this story. Wondjina believe that dream-time is cosmological time, the principal order of all things to exist in the universe. It's believed some versions of these paintings do not contain mouths otherwise it would continue to rain without relief. Maybe in those versions, mouths were omitted to mark silent moments, or the mouths themselves did not receive a new coat of paint at some point. Or, the lack of a mouth could have a significant meaning to Aborigines which we have yet to decipher.

Relics from the past portray imagery, at times, which some people consider exclusive to modern technology and the modern world.

Spirituality

With an open mind one can see human history is shrouded in mystery without logical explanations. These occurrences are not just limited to our past as they happen on a daily basis. Sometimes these events are disregarded for they may seem inconsequential at the time. Most importantly, the growing collective of events both past and present are working to open our consciousness, letting us know that we are a part of something bigger and greater than any of us could ever imagine.

Throughout history we find clues to who our ancestors were and who they are now as their legends live strong. Its easy to look back and imagine the past as a picture, but the true scope of events happened over time is always more than a million words have to offer.

Found within this section are subjects with a substantial following even-though little or no widely accepted physical evidence exists. Stories passed down from generation to generation are a large part of who we are. The points of origin aren't specifically known yet a large portion of modern society believes in their existence, or has heard the concepts before.

Hard physical evidence which has not been discovered might really exist in some form or another. Conspiracy theorists tend to suggest physical evidence is lacking because it's locked away from the public and only privy to those on Earth in very powerful positions. This is further elaborated into a grand master scheme whereby seven billion people are controlled by a select few individuals with all the right connections to make it happen.

In one respect, a small group of people controlling an entire planet seems plausible considering resources are largely governed by monetary systems, and hence the ties to central bank involvement. However, and as demonstrated time and time again throughout the ages, money itself may eventually become an archaic sense of organization and turn into a long forgotten hyper-reality as mankind travels further into the universe. Vessels traveling through the cosmos will require resources, not money, to operate and survive.

Then, there we are, deep within the dark abyss of the universe. Who shall we turn to then? *Each other, and our spiritual connections to the universal mind.*

Divine Astronauts

Belief in absolutely any religion or supernatural existence is acceptance of a concept larger than any mind is capable of comprehending. Implications of a discovery providing scientific proof of a religious existence is quite astonishing to say the least and nearly every culture around the world shares common belief in profound ideas that tie humanity to a spiritual world and the universe. Several basic concepts link cultures together even-though each individual religion differs from one to the next.

Countless belief systems refer to beings from "up above" coming down to visit Earth to pass on knowledge and values. There must be some sort of significance to the traditional sense of heavens resting in the skies above toward Earth's atmosphere towards space. Ancient cultures have passed down star knowledge throughout the ages. In fact, so many ancient civilizations depended on the stars for navigation and crop schedules that they created monuments and chiseled charts into stone describing them.

The part which seems too interesting to ignore or pass on as just a coincidence; It's evident ancient cultures focused on the stars, planets, and the sky above with respect to beliefs more than the land they lived upon. Why? Back then people could walk or swim or boat for miles and miles, but according to historical record they could not fly. It's not unreasonable to believe enormous stairways were built given the situation and an overwhelming urge to discover what resides in the heavens above.

Suppose an ancient culture became so determined to touch the sky that they built enormous structures in attempt to reach it. Looking up toward space is very deceiving and the optical illusion managed to trick scholars time and time again. If it was believed possible to build a stairway to the heavens then the evidence of such a feat now rests around the world.

Archeology explains a very different and intriguing story with respect to the world's largest unexplainable monuments. Many gigantic sites have been deemed sacred by cultures who are credited to the mind-boggling constructions. Often these large stone structures are identified as tombs, holy sanctuaries, and even altars for sacrificial ceremonies. Together the monuments share a link to the culture who is believed responsible for the construction and to that culture's belief system. Although the religious beliefs differ from culture to culture as the stone structures do, the similarities between them are quite incredible to say the least.

J.C. Vintner

Suppose each ancient civilization was once visited in the distant past by a being from another location in the universe. Imagine the impact such an event would have on a culture. Most likely it would define and shape the belief system of the civilization while becoming part of everyday life as an accepted part of the past, especially if the visitation altered how the culture lives on a daily basis with technology and otherworldly knowledge. The potential of such a situation might even create a brand new religion from scratch.

Proponents of Ancient Alien theories suggest several cultures have been visited in the past by ancient astronauts who passed on knowledge of the universe. If this is the case, given potential religious impact, then also imagine the possibility of multiple otherworldly beings visiting Earth and interacting with multiple ancient cultures, lets say perhaps one for each known religion. It begins to suggest why there is a the great diversity between religious beliefs world-wide although each sharing common characteristics.

This concept also suggests why certain religions feud with each other just as the alien visitors might have. Religions pride themselves in specific attention to detail when it comes to the duties of an individual and the feats Gods have performed when compared by belief systems. The principal line, though, is that all religions and all related cultures *believe in something greater than themselves.*

An excellent rebuttal to the births of numerous religions being inspired from ancient astronauts is tied to basic primitive instincts of humans. Mankind is competitive by nature in the eye of survival. Before modern advancements in technology societies were more dependent on hunter-gatherer skills necessary to provide food and shelter on a daily basis. This helped define a seemingly healthy competitive behavior to be the best provider while ensuring the bloodline of the best survivors transcends generations.

Competition with increasing population helped force humans to develop a more stubborn outlook on daily life in order to maintain self-confidence and mask any self-doubts. A complementary aspect to ancient foraging societies is evidence from African bush tribes of ceremonies performed to bring food from a successful hunt along with help from domesticated dogs. Years later similar ceremonies continued though in focus to bring rain to nurture crops as the past foraging turned into an agricultural base by domesticating corn and wheat.

Beliefs that natural process is influenced by prayers, meditations, and ceremonies could become quite rooted in the limbic system as a conditioned response, especially if they continuously provide positive results over several generations. Perhaps discrepancies between spiritual beliefs are a long-term outcome of ancient society's persistence to be stubbornly competitive in the name of survival.

Whether or not mankind's ancient ancestors were once visited by beings from space the fact remains that Earth's ancient people were heavily influenced in their day to day lives by changes in the cosmos. It's very possible those changes effected timing for crop seasons and migration periods throughout the world and it's evident these patterns were recorded to help facilitate the cycle of life for ancient man. Cosmic events continue to play predominate role in society's daily life just as it did throughout the ages. Increases in technological capability have brought more attention to the possibility of life outside of Earth than ever before. Skeptics are faced with much greater challenges to disprove in the vast wealth of information accumulation over the past century.

Mathematics demonstrates probability of life existing on other planets to be much more common than ever imagined. Biological research in the deep ocean and other formidably hostile environments on Earth provide evidence of life thriving in areas which defy all sense of life's fragility. Space explorations are constantly searching for life's building blocks on planetary bodies and are now developing methods to focus on theorized habitable zones around stars in distant galaxies. Quantum theories suggest life may even exist closer to Earth and could possibly be accessed by entering a parallel dimension.

The discovery of life (outside of planet Earth) in the universe is an inevitable event in mankind's future which it must be prepared to acknowledge. Currently it's unclear if the probability of life means finding a form of intelligent being capable of communicating with humans, or if it reveals a form of primitive life resembling ancient insects from mankind's evolutionary time-line.

Adding a bit of quantum wonderment into the idea of discovering life elsewhere in the universe purposes that the life could be a product of anything and everything imaginable which further justifies a cautious approach. Early 20th century science fiction stories are a great indication of the human imagination's idea of possible forms life could evolve into. This does not mean life from other planets would necessarily be hostile toward mankind, but it does require consideration for any space ventures throughout the cosmos.

A planet far away with gigantic amoebas who only gorge on anything in their path to grow larger and larger seems very unlikely yet quantum science suggests plausible scenarios given a planet with all the right environmental variables to produce such a living creature. The point is simply this. As mankind travels further way from Earth in search for extraterrestrial life, it must become increasingly capable of expecting the unexpected while adapting quickly and efficiently.

Angels

Cherubs and Angels are an integral part of many cultural belief systems world-wide. Society consistently associates angelic beings divinely with the heavens. The name is derived from the Greek, Angelos, meaning messenger, though many of the ancient Semitic languages such as Hebrew and Aramaic refer to Angels as Malak. In ancient Sumerian culture, archangels were those who fell to Earth following a war in the heavens. When closely examined, there is a significant relation between the naming of the archangels. They commonly share the suffix "EL" specifically referring to the title of "Angel." According to research, the suffix is not limited to archangel name designations.

The appearance of an Angel is something nearly anyone is able to describe without discrepancy. Feathers and wings are common elements among Angelic deities in several cultures who combine the idea of flight with the flesh of a human. Egyptian God Horus and Goddesses Maat and Isis are normally represented with focus to their wings. Assyrian God Ashur, the Greek Gods Eros, Boreas, Goddesses Iris and Nike; Sumerian Gods Nephilim, Elohim, the Anunnaki, Ninhursag, and Faravahar. The number of winged deities stretches well beyond those made famous or documented in historical record. Feathered wings are depicted on beings and objects considered divine in most cultures.

Essentially, there are many interpretations of types of Angels differing from culture to culture. Guardian Angels who protect and help guide in one belief system, may also be Writing Angels in another, who write good and bad deeds down for later judgment. There are the Watchers and the Fallen, and several other distinct roles an Angel may assume depending on the associated belief system and its circumstances. The bottom line remains though, the very idea of an Angel transcends many cultural belief systems.

Holy Grail

Known as the cup Jesus drank from during the Last Supper, the sacred Holy Grail is arguably the most sought after religious artifact next to the Ark of the Covenant. Legends of the Grail's existence have steadily grown over the centuries by ongoing quests to locate it. Some have even speculated the term Holy Grail is really a metaphor and doesn't refer to a physical object. Still, many have searched in hope they may have a chance to hold the most divine of sacred relics. Popular theories base the Grail's location as secretive, passed down from generation to generation, changing hands only when necessary.

Officially endorsed by the Roman Catholic Church, The Knights Templar have long been suspected of knowing where the Holy Grail is kept. Rumors have placed the Knights in key locations during the Crusades. Individuals claim to have witnessed Templar Knights digging and searching for something while in the Temple Mount. These stories have long tied the Templar to relics like the Holy Grail, Ark of the Covenant and the Shroud of Turin. Theories suggest when the Holy Land was lost, many Templar faced persecution and several went into hiding along with the relics they were said to be protecting. It's believed the Order's efforts to keep the relics a secret were very extensive, to the point of using cryptic messages in communication and elaborately constructed buildings to hide them in. Many stories about the quest for the Holy Grail often involve decoding signs and messages left behind by the Knights Templar.

Prominent structures like Rosslyn Chapel and Oak Island are believed to be secretly housing the Holy Grail or the Ark of the Covenant. Either location would make an excellent hideaway, yet conclusive historical evidence is lacking to place either relic in those locations. Many relics and valuable items have been buried for protection in the past and it is not out of the question to think those hiding the Holy Grail would have worked extra diligently to keep it from falling into the wrong hands.

Tree of Life

Many ancient civilizations share similar creation stories including a representative form known as the Tree of Life. Some cultures envision the Tree of Life to exhibit the circular flow of creation from the divine to Earth and back, while others simply see it as directions for humanity to travel back to the heavens.

Further beliefs represent different levels of consciousness and our subjective experiences while traveling along different paths. However the Tree of Life is looked at, the fundamental principals seem to remain consistent. The design is considered to be one of the most recognizable and most scared shape in sacred geometry, believed to form the key to all of creation.

Modern science uses a forms of the Tree of Life throughout several disciplines, usually as a basis to demonstrate the process of evolution, classify animals and geological matter. Genealogy utilizes the concept to trace human relatives back to their ancestors. Versions of the Caduceus and Rod of Asclepius symbolized in medicine reflect a serpent coiled around the Tree of Life. Biology adapts a form in phylogenetics to construct an evolutionary tree relating various groups of organisms together. Regardless of how diagrams and symbols are applied to the sciences, the Tree of Life helps humanity visualize interconnected and related elements in a tangible form.

Lost Ark of the Covenant

Prophet Jeremiah spoke of a time when the land is filled with people, the Ark of the Covenant will no longer be talked about. Even the thought of the Ark would not enter anyone's mind. Present day seems to follow suit with the land being filled, but there are many who still talk about, research, and are trying to find the Ark. According to a vision on Mount Sinai, God commanded Moses to construct the Ark of the Covenant to house the sacred tablets of the ten commandments.

Biblical accounts may suggest the Ark provided direct communication with God especially in situations where it's documented to have a great deal of power over conflict. The book of Joshua talks about the destruction of Jericho by rams' horns after the Ark was paraded around the city for seven days. Also, the river Jordan was parted by the presence of the Ark.

Several accounts, and some found in the Bible, describe the adverse affects the Ark, almost as if though it might have been radioactive on some level. In the book of Samuel there is specific reference to people begging Philistine rulers to send the Ark back to its own country before it kills everyone, as the hand of the Lord was heavy and devastated the people of Ashdod with tumors. Further references claim those who touched the Ark died instantly or shortly thereafter.

The last known resting place on record is believed to have been around 650 BCE, at Herod's second Temple in Jerusalem. A copper scroll found in 1952 near the same cave area as the Dead Sea Scrolls suggests the Ark was among the sacred objects listed to reside in the Temple until its 70 CE destruction. Similar to the Holy Grail, many have searched meticulously in hopes of discovering the Ark. Studies of the mysterious tunnel system on Oak Island have revealed elevated levels of radiation suggesting the reason for building such an elaborate hydraulic system was to protect and hide the Ark of the Covenant.

Shroud of Turin

Subjected to modern science, the Shroud of Turin might be the single most studied and scrutinized object believed to be a sacred relic from the time of Christ. The linen appears to be the burial shroud wrapped around Jesus after crucifixion. Several theories believe it to be the work of a previously unknown artistic process. Unanimously, the question of how the image was formed and survived on the Shroud hasn't been answered. A new controversial theory places the Shroud in the hands of the Knights Templar after

1204 CE and that it's actually possible to read the burial certificate of Jesus on the Shroud itself. Should this theory hold true, the mystery will again deepen with further questioning, examination and scrutiny.

Light and the Divine Halo

Floating discs often depicted behind or above the face of a divine being in a bursting golden color are commonly believed to represent light, glory, and dawning in religious context. Yet a halo at first glance with no prior knowledge, seems to simply resemble the shining sun, similar to the solar disc Egyptian god Ra is usually shown with. Ra combines all aspects as that of the sun to science, as a necessity for life, bringer of warmth and growth.

Upon closer inspection, the solar disc is not just imagery of the sun, as it is also wrapped with a serpent coil called a Kundalini; This is representative of potential energy rising to open the Chakras, on the path to rebirth - As the sun does each day. The halo in Egyptian reliefs depicts a life-giving sun, and appears to signify this more than designations to Ra as glorious or divine as those aspects are implied as part of the nature of Ra, the god of the sun. Religions other than Egyptian tend to utilize this iconography to identify individual glory, the light, and divinity.

In Buddhism, a colorful circular disc emanates from the body of Buddha after achieving enlightenment. A halo's color of light symbolizes the level of spiritual elevation, similar to the rising and setting sun, as the sun appears to change the sky's color throughout the day. Sunlight in its purest form is white, containing a full spectrum of colors, of which only certain wavelengths are visible depending on the current atmospheric conditions.

Enlightenment is a gentle awakening of conscious energy, a way of connecting to the universal mind, becoming whole with nature and the divine. This idea of self-realization frees an individual from bounds of consciousness when awakened, opening the mind to a new world.

To many people, prominence of the halo is most recognized from Christian artworks dating back as far as the 4th century to designate the divine. Essentially this element commonly found in religious artwork was an interpretation of light and glory emanating outward. The halo often appears like the sun is located directly behind the head, mimicking its power and life-giving nature. Even-though light travels on a dimensional plane, artworks tend to depict the halo as a flat disc. Like Buddhism, these icons represent a level of divinity, imbued with the energy of God. The bible refers to the halo growing in size during Christ's transfigurations in prophet revelations, another key aspect to reaching enlightenment.

Modern ancient alien theories about the halo point in a different direction, contending the circular disc of light is actually representative of an ancient astronaut helmet in a simplistic sense, like looking at a bubble over someone's head face-on. Perhaps this means our ancestors were ancient astronauts themselves yet...

Somehow alien astronaut theory neglects the related stories, legends, and modern enlightenment practices still thriving today in this sense; The foundation of why our ancestors encircled heads of the divine with an all powerful light similar to the sun. This points to a greater likeliness, as in the case of ancient aliens, Earth was once visited by beings from another world who were capable of emanating light outward from their heads, and mankind interpreted this in representation as those beings as divine from the heavens, since they indeed descended from up above.

Georgia Guidestones

Located in Elbert County Georgia, a mysterious anonymously funded project stands tall, known as the Georgia Guidestones, or American Stonehenge. The Elberton Granite Finishing company built the pyramid blue granite structure in 1980 per funding from a person going by the name of R.C. Christian.

Theories link the interesting pseudonym to Rosicrucianism along with parts of the text found inscribed on the stones. It's believed the content is a sort of guideline for the future conservation of mankind, but the basis has not yet been deciphered. In addition to ten guidelines inscribed in eight different languages, the stones themselves are orientated and aligned to mark the 18.6 year lunar declination cycle, as well as the Sun solstices and equinoxes. The inscriptions found on the pyramid blue stone structure read as follows.

1. *Maintain humanity under 500,000,000 in perpetual balance with nature*
2. *Guide reproduction wisely, improving fitness and diversity*
3. *Unite humanity with a living new language*
4. *Rule passion, faith, tradition, and all things with tempered reason*
5. *Protect people and nations with fair laws and just courts*
6. *Let all nations rule internally resolving external disputes in a world court*
7. *Avoid petty laws and useless officials*
8. *Balance personal rights with social duties*
9. *Prize truth, beauty, love, seeking harmony with the infinite*
10. *Be not a cancer on the earth, leave room for nature*

The cap-stone manages to keep track of the current day of the year with a sun ray passing through and provides a direct peering hole at Polaris. A key-guide tablet can be found a short distance from the guide-stones with an inscription referring to the burial of a time capsule below.

J.C. Vintner

Holy Spear

Known as the Spear of Destiny, the Holy Lance is believed to have pierced the side of Jesus by Cassius Longinus. According to historical tracking, the Holy Spear has followed a long circular route, changing hands with many influential leaders through many dire situations, back to its resting place in Nuremberg, Germany. Though four lances have claimed to have touched Christ, one in particular stands apart due to recent technological examination.

The Vienna Lance, or Hofburg spear, was subjected to an array of tests which resulted in startling revelations to its origin. Inside the inscribed wrappings layered around the broken spear, a length of metal was found in the shape of a crucifixion nail. The nail is decorated in tiny cross marks which originally caught the eye of the examiners. Further investigation revealed traces of cobalt dating to the time of Christ, accurately within tolerance. Each of the layers and inscriptions were carefully studied, identifying the owner at the time who placed the wrappings which also date respectively. The story of the Vienna Lance corroborates the results of the existing physical evidence, suggesting it to be housing one of the only known relics to have survived to this day from the crucifixion.

Miracle of Fatima

Three young girls tending sheep in 1917, near their home village in Fatima Portugal, described an encounter with a woman who appeared to them, brighter than the sun. The glowing woman identified herself as the Lady of the Rosary and told the girls to pray on the rosary every day, that it is the key to personal and world peace. Two other visits to the girls were claimed to happen at Cova da Iria. One visit became known as the Miracle of the Sun when roughly 70,000 people gathered to witness the sun rotating and appearing to change colors like a dance.

The strange phenomenon was distinctly witnessed by more than 10,000 of the attendees and reported up to 40 miles away. Scientific speculations of the event claim the color changing and dancing sun to be symptoms of looking into the sun for too long due to retinal damage. Another theory proposes an increase in atmospheric interference extending the typical sightings of aurora borealis beyond their common locations. One such event was documented in 1938, shortly after a prediction from Fatima as a sign foretelling a grim future. Some believe this sign to be relevant to forthcoming events of Hitler seizing Austria one month later, and the Czech invasion eight months later.

Dead Sea Scrolls

Nearly 1,000 previously unknown texts were discovered in a series of caves marked as the ruins of ancient Qumran on the northwest shore of the Dead Sea. Considered the oldest known surviving Biblical texts, particular interest in the mysterious Dead Sea Scrolls to Ancient Alien theorists is the Divine Throne-Chariot script. Inspired by the books of Ezekiel and Revelation, the Divine Throne-Chariot is described as a Merkabah, both supported and drawn by cherubim. Each cherubim is credited for making a little noise as it folds wings though the Bible does not mention this at all in Kings.

The area below the throne seat is described to have turning wheels where angels come and go coupled with an array of beautiful colors. As the Throne-Chariot is indeed written as the vehicle of God, the descriptions definitely seem to build a picture of an ancient flying device using the context available to our ancestors at the time. Furthermore, literature on the Merkabah is scarce because the subject was forbidden in the Mishnah to share any understanding of the Merkabah with anyone who was less knowledgeable.

Life is full of puzzles and secrets for some of which we may not quite understand.

J.C. Vintner

Spiritual Advocates

Two of the most highly controversial
subjects presented in daily topics of discussion in
our modern age are politics and religion, partially
due a number of borderline beliefs attached to
each discipline known to have ulterior motives.
Generally both make claims to provide society
with a better life, yet both have their own methods
of obtaining money, ensuring survival of the
organization in known or unknown ways.

Not all politics or religions are corrupt
however, many of the participators do mean well
in the progress of society, but do they understand
how actions can affect the world negatively? Both
promise solutions to problems created by greed,
corruption and deception, even-though the very
foundations they're built upon are flawed. When
drawing comparisons between religion and
politics we find similarities because religions such
as Christianity exemplify spiritual political
practice.

Organized churches, like politics, rely on
being an authority of truth to maintain power.
From this position they're able to bend or change
truths, or utilize a selective retention process to
hide truths for benefit of the establishment. The
biggest red flag should be that both religion and

politics are quick to point out what's wrong, why it's wrong, and how their solution is the best solution to fix the problem.

Arguing in any political or religious debate becomes gruesomely exhausting because suggestive ideas are usually shot down instantaneously, being completely wrong from the first word, since they are not in line with ideal correct methods of thought in that particular individual's representative belief system. If the truth was truly desired, both religion and politics would not have to desperately find ways to prove their perception of what's right.

We know literary works throughout the ages have been translated, modified, fine tuned, and altered to facilitate their purpose in commerce. Unless the writings are etched into old rocks, metal sheets, or even wood, it's difficult to prove passages from the Bible haven't been altered. Romans rewrote several parts of the testaments and omitted any messages which weren't suitable to the Roman government's way of life on multiple occasions.

Rulers in Rome often relied on fear mongering tactics for maintaining power over the masses by spectacles of violence, torturing, and dismembering. Those who didn't follow the rules were not only subject to these punishments, but were also made examples of during by being put on public display for crowds to cheer and harass. When Rome realized the power and wealth attributed to the Bible they adopted and modified it for exploitation of resources through psychological fear mongering with Christianity.

True premeditated hypocrisy is found in messages conveyed by various passages found throughout the Bible, completely intentional design. Corrupt religions often depict a warm, happy place on the outside as a method of attraction while hiding sinister motives from prying accusations. They will deliver us from our sins, from everything we've ever done wrong in their eyes, and protect us from the evils who intend to harm us.

Convince the public there is something out of their control they should be afraid of, then step in to become their savior and reap the benefits. Bad religion acts as spiritual politicians and advocates of the supreme creator all for the sole purpose of pilfering commitment as loyal donations. Arguably, the Roman Church is a place of business where people pay for spiritual comfort while disguised as the human authoritative of a divine creator. The wolf in sheep's clothing who acts righteous in the face of man while squandering money, power, and resources, with the empire being a shameless, shallow, artificial version of true nature's spirituality.

Stories in the Bible find roots in older belief systems dating well before the time of Jesus and the birth of the age of Pisces. Along with cuneiform script carvings left by ancient Sumerian, relief carvings found in the Luxor Temple of Egypt almost exactly describe the same stories written in the Bible yet date to a time almost 3,000 years before the crucifixion.

The ten commandments were borrowed, nearly for word, from the Book of the Dead, carved well before the time of Moses.

Egyptian beliefs attribute the bringing of light, heat, and growth to Sun God Ra and his battle with the underworld. Linking symbolism in the Bible to Egyptian myth stories brings up extremely interesting coincidences especially considering the fact that traditional beliefs in Ra died out during the rise of Christianity.

They didn't really disappear, instead they were transformed as the age of Aries ended and Pisces began while ushering in Christianity, Islam and Buddhism. If you look at key passages in the Bible and replace Son (as in Jesus) to the literal sense, Sun (as in Ra), interpretations of the text become much more profound and logical. For example, the sun of God was able to walk on water. As the sun sets over water its reflection appears in a narrow line which becomes marginally smaller the further the sun goes down, giving the impression it's walking on rippling water.

Apply this concept to John 3:16, God (the creator) gave his one and only Sun and those who believe in him will have everlasting life, believe in Ra and you will have everlasting life. Have a look at Hebrews 1:3 next. The Sun is the radiance (of light) of God's glory, the exact representation of his being, sustaining all things by his powerful word, where the word is life; John 1:14 the word became flesh and lived among us. Another intriguing resemblance happens on a daily basis as Sun comes down to Earth from the heavens at sunset and resurrects from Earth at sunrise, the very same daily battle described in the Luxor relief carving.

Ancient Locations

All over the world there are massively impressive megaliths, monoliths, and other stone structures seeming to defy modern logic. Countless theories try explaining how they were built and for what purpose. These gigantic creations have reshaped the way we think of our ancestors and their past capabilities. Other theories suggest it is assumed that many cultures used primitive tools to shape and move giant blocks.

The question we must ask is not why they would build them, as purposed in History Channel's Ancient Aliens series, but why would our ancestors build on an enormous, complicated scale? It's understood the importance of the Gods and the honor in pleasing them. Common sense leads one to believe that our ancestors would've built in the manor if it were easy to do. New-age theorists and Alien Astronaut proponents propose ideas pushing boundaries beyond brute-force manpower by numbers to simple yet effective techniques, possibly learned from the Gods themselves.

Scientists have established theories for several mysterious locations based on archaeological findings and historical records which indicate potential methods our ancestors might have used. The problem with most sites is a strange lacking of tools believed to be used for moving rocks weighing upward of 400-500 tons. Elaborate winch and pulley mechanisms are suspect for some cases, as some evidence in the Great Pyramid of Giza suggests. Not one piece found so far can explain exactly how these sites were constructed.

Couple with this, the known facts that many of these megalithic building cultures lived at opposite ends of the world, or during different periods in history. This concept places our ancestors more likely to have been isolated from each other than to have interacted and shared their cultural beliefs. Few ancient trade routes have been discovered and some of the furthest known distances materials were transported range from 1,500 to 2,000 miles. We're talking over 9,000 miles if a plane flew relatively straight point A to B, from Egypt to visit Palenque. Yet evidence such as herbs only found in South America have been found buried with some Pharaohs, indicating these two cultures may have interacted directly at some point.

Multiple cultures around the world were able to build with such precision, on such an enormous scale, with so many strikingly similar features that it gives the distinct impression they must have interacted in some way. Building upwards may also have spiritual significance as the structures bring one closer to the heavens, even so far as to offering the soul a pathway to follow into the afterlife.

One might look at the pyramids in this way and think, what if the true purpose of a pyramid was not only to offer the soul a channel of passage, but what if literally they're a stairway to the heavens, and during a time science understands people were not flying. One of the greatest curiosities back then, without flight, had to be discovering what resides in the space above Earth. Perhaps building one pyramid was not enough to reach the edge, so another was built taller, and then another.

It's a great motivation to thousands upon thousands of pyramid builders around the world, to say they are helping to build a pathway into the heavens, to touch the sun and the moon. Looking up into the sky is deceiving and even with modern technology it's difficult to truly comprehend those 248.514 miles between the Earth's surface and space, let alone trying to reach the moon, sun, and stars. Giza is 0.0863706 miles tall, meaning the Egyptians needed to build a structure 2,877 times the size; then only to discover a seemingly endless vacuum of space.

Maybe structures around the world first met with primitive attempts to travel into the heavens, and without flight capability this sounds quite plausible, though perhaps in time we may discover an alternate means for traversing the universe directly from Earth's surface.

Easter Island

Discovered in the South Pacific Ocean on the Easter Sunday of 1722, Easter Island is widely known today for the very large freestanding megalithic Moai watching over the island. Nearly 900 unique Moai carbon date to between 1100 and 1680 with an estimation of a year or more of work per statue. Each Moai is said to resemble the deceased head of an ancestor. Many of the of the massive 80 ton statues were chiseled from volcanic ash, remnant from the extinct volcanoes which originally formed the island. Methods of moving and lifting the Moai into place have remained an unexplained, controversial mystery. The Moai are astronomically aligned precisely with seven 18 ton statues pointing directly to the sun setting during the equinox, named for the Seven Sisters or Pleiades.

Polynesians who inhabited Easter Island between 300 and 800CE chose a representative of MakeMake, the great creator. Each year the appointed Bird Man is sent to live in seclusion to appease MakeMake. Effigies of the Bird Man resemble a human with a bird head and wings distinctly similar to depictions found in the ancient Egyptian culture.

Stonehenge

World famous Stonehenge is located in Wiltshire, United Kingdom. Estimates date the first primitive structure to around 8,000 BCE, from examining the remaining Mesolithic post-holes. Archaeological evidence suggests three distinct constructions with three major amendments between 3,100 BCE and 1,600 BCE progressing from light timber to stone structures weighing between five and forty tons. Speculations ranging from how Stonehenge was constructed, to its specific purpose are still ongoing to present day.

J.C. Vintner

Reason for the mystery boils down to one astonishing fact apart from other megalithic structures. Stonehenge was built by a culture who did not leave a known written record behind. The only evidence left in the area of those who used the site appears to be found in the form of over 500 barrows populated with human bones. Theories claim the area was used for either sacrificial or healing rituals with no other logical explanation for the highly concentrated grave site.

Study over the years revealed intriguing findings suggesting that Stonehenge is an ancient astronomical calendar. Alignments between the massive stones coincide with the summer and winter solstice, the equinox and moon phases. Recent archaeoastronomical theory combines the alignment with supporting bone evidence found at the henge and nearby sites. The results establish that Stonehenge was only used during the winter solstice each year with no clear evidence to place anyone at the site during summer months.

Nazca

Found in the desert of Peru, the Nazca Lines contain large scale geoglyphs which seem to only make sense by looking at them from the air high above. The nature of the glyphs leads one to believe the Nasca who inhabited the area between 200 BCE and 700 CE were either flying themselves or witnessed others flying, if they were the geoglyph creators. Over 15,000 animal shapes and geometric patterns fill the relatively flat landscape including formations that appear to be runways or landing strips.

Since the desert in Nazca is mainly composed of rock and stone material, the creation process involved removing the top layer over several miles to create each glyph.   The precision is matched with an equally accurate solar positioning. Several glyphs point directly to celestial locations.

Also located in Peru, not terribly far from the Nazca Lines, one can find an unexplained Band of Holes on the Cajamarquilla plain. An estimated 6,900 man-sized holes carved into the stone stretch the plain, with no related archaeological evidence found to date. From the air, the Band of Holes distinctly looks like a machine drove over the land for a few miles. Scientists presume the area is the result of an unknown geological process.

Cambay Ruins

Ancient cities discovered off the coast of Cambay in India demonstrate remarkable building capabilities of an ancient people using giant granite blocks described to be fit together like sugar cubes. Two sites found date as far back as 7,500 BCE with one turning up pre-Harappan artifacts. Fifteen miles away, the second site known as the lost ruins of Mahabaliipuram, features a completely different architectural style, lacks any sort of artifacts found as the first, and has not revealed any inscriptions to help identify it. Controversy over both sites dismisses wooden pieces recovered by dredging and claims the pottery shards found do not show any signs of being Harappan, that they must be natural formation otherwise known as geofacts.

Underwater images of the sites reveal distinct man-made structures believed to be the ancient cities of Khambhat and Dwarka. There is a legend found in an ancient Sanskrit text describing Lord Krishna leaving Earth after a great battle with UFOs and the city of Dwarka sinking into the sea.

Okinawa & Yonaguni

Off the coast of Yonaguni Island, Japan, resides a most impressive underwater structure with staircases and sharp-cornered flat terraces. Ongoing debates are trying to pinpoint if the massive structure is man-made or formed from natural processes on slate rock. Several features including what appears to be a piece of Kaida script were discovered, but carbon dating seems to put the structure at a time possibly around 1,000 BCE, when the sea level closely resembled that of today.

An original estimate dated the site to 8,000 BCE at a time when the site would've been above water. Though debates suggest Yonaguni to be a natural formation, those same geologists believe that it's quite possible that it may have been modified by humans in the past. The problem with a natural erosive process at Yonaguni is that no fragments have been found supporting the theory.

Nearly 300 miles away in Okinawa, distinctly impressive step-like pyramids were discovered further bolstering the idea of human intervention at the Yonaguni site. This area is undoubtedly man-made with features such as archways, 90° corners, ceremonial flat terraced platforms, stone circles and hexagonal columns. Both sites can be found in comparable depth close to 100 ft. below the ocean's surface. Current theories suggest the Okinawa site as similar to a castle wall coherent in architecture to nearby locations whereas the Yonaguni site might be more of a ceremonial platform.

J.C. Vintner

Bermuda Triangle & Devil's Sea

Navy bomber Flight 19, a group of five pilots on a training mission over the Atlantic, suddenly disappeared without a trace in an area now known as the Bermuda Triangle. Authors during the time published stories, articles, and books steadily bringing attentions to the mysterious happenings in and around the triangle. The articles outlining strange disappearances soon featured a triangular drawing on a map in attempt to triangulate missing vessel and aircraft locations. The triangle now is believed by some to not show any more strange disappearances than any other part of the ocean. Others believe there is substantial non-embellished evidence credible to previous conclusive statements that the Bermuda Triangle is a strange unexplained anomaly.

Airplanes and ships passing through the area do occasionally report compass malfunctions, instrument panel problems, and slight disorientation which could be responsible for mishaps along with human error. A compass will naturally and normally shift at times to fix on the magnetic bearing but this does not account for sporadic spinning coupled with electronic components losing power. Physical anomalies have not been identified in the triangle though other possible causes have been attributed to hurricanes, methane hydrate fields, rogue waves and even the gulf stream.

Recent theories contest the Bermuda Triangle and similar locations found around the world are products of anomalies and fluctuations in the Earth's magnetic field. Hot spots for these areas of anomalies and unexplained phenomena were dubbed Vile Vortices by Ivan T. Sanderson. Strangely enough, another dangerous triangle exists south of Tokyo in the Pacific Ocean, called the Devil's Sea or Dragon's Triangle, not very far from Okinawa and Yonaguni.

Japanese maps specifically report the area to be a danger zone having lost hundreds of crew members on several ships over the years. Both the Bermuda Triangle and Dragon's Triangle have reports dating to the 1950s, which were equally publicized in their respective areas except Japanese legends from 1,000 BCE describe dragons living off the coast of Japan.

Gobekli Tepe

Uncovered near Sanliurfa, Turkey, the earliest known ancient ruins called Gobekli Tepe carbon dates to ~9,000 BCE and features carvings and a language that might be the earliest known form of writing. The ruins are formed in rings of megalithic blocks estimated to weigh seven to fifty tons each. Every stone is intricately carved with animal figures. Theorists state the megaliths were placed by piling sand up then making a platform. Further theories suggest the opposite, that these megaliths were purposely buried in order to hide them, or blowing sands over the years covered the site up. It's estimated another fifty years of digging could finally uncover all of the ruins at this location. So far there are no sources explaining what the symbolic language means or who was responsible for creating Gobekli Tepe. There is an especially significant find at Gobekli. Archaeologists discovered a small sphinx with the distinct characteristics of another world famous sphinx replicated nearly 7,000 years later in Egypt on a grand scale.

Atlantis

The only existing written records referring to Atlantis are Plato's 360 BC dialogs Timaeus and Critias. In the dialogs, Critias and Timaeus entertain Socrates with a story that is "not a fiction, but true." Timaeus describes the creation of the world and explains natural phenomena while Critias talks of a lost island, its people and ancient Athenians.

Briefly mentioned in the Timaeus dialog, Critias talks of Poseidon possessing the island of Atlantis. The island is described having a very fertile plain and "not very high mountain" in the center. Two springs, one warm and one cold. The extremity facing the country of Gadeirus. An abundance of wood and a great number of elephants. Bridges over the seas which surrounded and parted the ancient metropolis with a road directly to the royal palace. A harbor and docks on the outer zone for sea passage. A zone cut from the sea, then a zone of equal land, a zone of water and land and one surrounding the central island. Quarried white, black and red stone built walls, towers and buildings.

Each zone wall is coated; The outside most wall in brass, the next with tin, and the third (citadel wall) with orichalcum which is thought to be a gold-copper alloy tumbaga. Around the temple were golden statues of the 10 kings and their wives. The two springs fed aqueducts along the bridges to the outer zones, distributing water along the way.

In the center of larger of the two islands, apart from the center Temple of Poseidon island, a race course for horses extended around the perimeter. All surrounded by a level plain, surrounded by mountains descending toward the sea, oblong in shape. Canals were cut and interconnected from the mountains to the city of which wood and fruits were transported. At the end of the known Critias dialog, Zues gathers all of the Gods into their most holy habitation placed in the center of the world for a speech. The remaining Critias dialog was lost or never written and there is no evidence of what Zues spoke to the Gods.

Atlantis is arguably the most prominent story of the ages. Many explorers have tried to uncover the location to show the world a most profound discovery. Some theories even suggest the island will rise from the sea in the time of Armageddon. Ancient underwater ruins found in several places across the globe continuously spark the question whether or not they're a part of the legend of Atlantis. Sources are credible but findings are inconclusive. The hunt continues and one day the island once described in Plato's dialogs might prove to be "not a fiction, but true."

The city of Pavlopetri off the shore of Laconia, Greece is believed by some as Plato's inspiration for his dialogs speaking of Atlantis. Pavlopetri is the oldest submerged city discovered and investigated thoroughly. The site contains many examples of buildings found in the Greek mainland. It's believed the city was home to royalty, gods, and heroes from evidence uncovered throughout the 30,000 square mile site.

Estimations date Pavlopetri to around 2,800 BCE and 1,100 BCE during the Bronze Age. The problem so far with claiming Pavlopetri to be the Atlantis Plato spoke of, is that the structures and landscape found do not resemble those described clearly in the dialogs

Angkor Wat

Built to honor Vishnu between 800-1100 CE, and believed to be a replica of the home of gods, the ancient Angkor Wat is one of the largest religious temples in the world. Of the five large towers, the central tower is said to represent Mount Meru, where Shiva resides at the center of the world according to Hindu mythology. There are 108 lotus bud shaped towers, a sacred number to both Hindi and Buddhists. More impressive than the structure of the city itself are over 2,000 divine nymph figures called Asparas decorating the walls and towers.

Among the nymphs are bas-reliefs describing the Hindu legends including the ancient battles (some fought in the sky), the 32 hells, 37 heavens, and the creation myth Churning the Sea of Milk. This very large and elaborately constructed temple aligns with the constellation Draco of 10,500 BCE for the spring equinox. Attuned to the sun and moon, further studies have found the bas-relief to function as a marker for the days between winter and summer solstices, opening a gateway to further hidden cosmological meaning. Over five million tons of sandstone was quarried and transported 25 miles to construct Angkor Wat temple.

Phaistos

The ancient city of Phaistos found south-central on the island of Crete in Greece became famous with the discovery of a hieroglyphic disc dating to 1,700 BC. A total of 241 figures in 45 glyphs spiral around to the center for the disc. Theories regarding the disc range from a farmer's almanac to a story of the human journey. Given the nature of the content found inscribed on the disc, a unified theory has not been decided upon.

Illustrations seem to point toward a type of astronomical calendar, or Epagomenen as known by the Egyptians. The Minoan culture repeatedly used symbolism for the times of death and rebirth along the lines of Sacred Geometry. It is not out of the question to perceive the disc as a means to track the times of sacrificial days.

Further studies reveal the possibility of the Phaistos Disc having a direct relation to Thoth, Isis and Osiris. Depictions of 12 ethereal pyramids around one, form an hourglass and the illusion of time. Egypt's influence on ancient Greece is well documented and profound to say the least. Thoth is known to have invented many arts and musical instruments in Greece with a primary responsibility of guiding souls of the dead across the winding waterway on his wings.

El Dorado

Known as the legendary lost city of gold, El Dorado legends originated in the Muisca territory from Spaniards who were told of a ritual at Lake Guatavita. Treasures were thrown into the lake as offerings for the new king. Attempts to drain the lake for unimaginable wealth took place until finally abandoned after many of the workers died and nothing was found. Stories then developed over the ages transforming the idea of discarded wealth at the bottom of a lake into an entire lost city of gold. El Dorado became a fixation for many explorers, some who even lost their own life in pursuit of the ultimate treasure. Recent satellite technology is changing the notion of El Dorado being a mythical city with a discovery of over 200 earthworks found near Brazil's border to Bolivia. The remains hint at a sophisticated civilization inhabiting the area between 200-1283 CE though no evidence has been found designating it as the legendary lost city of gold.

J.C. Vintner

Ancient Egypt

The Great Pyramid of Egypt has presented an unexplained mystery from its very sight by the modern world. How were they built? A question which definitely extends beyond that of the Great Pyramid to several structures found world-wide. Egypt manages to tie the very question to the pyramids due to the monumental scale alone. Scope of such a project seems so inconceivable that our ancient ancestors would've accomplished such feats. Several theories have suggested plausible building methods that may have been used throughout Egyptian constructions. Solid and conclusive evidence has not been discovered. It's believed the granite used for building was transported from 580 miles away using the Nile River which includes slabs weighing up to eighty tons found in the burial chamber.

Debates continue to this day attempting to unravel the mystery behind the pyramids. It's widely understood the Egyptians built to please their kings and gods, and with honor during the process. What cannot be explained is why they decided to build with such magnitude and precision, unless of course it was easy for them to do. Modern archeology and modern science has not discovered any such process of moving giant stone blocks and it being easy for the Egyptians, but it doesn't necessarily mean any such evidence does not exist.

Karnak

Comparable to Angkor Wat in prominence and size, the Temple of Karnak at Luxor is currently believed to be the world's largest surviving religious structure. Pharaohs were considered gods and they required an area given the same attention as other gods. Karnak definitely fulfills this ideology. Gigantic pylons and statues adorn the temple symbolizing Karnak's physical residence and needs, including an obelisk weighing 328 tons. Attention to interior lighting effects is evident throughout the temple which exemplifies the focus on finely detailed craftsmanship. More recently, a 3,500 year old door to the afterlife was unearthed near the temple. Archaeologists claim it is a false door designed to allow the deceased and his wife to interact with the world of the living. Karnak is deemed one of the many god's mansions built specifically for political and religious purposes.

Sphinx of Giza

The earliest known Sphinx sculpture was discovered at Gobekli Tepe dating to roughly 9,500 CE nearly 7,000 years before the gigantic version was constructed on the Giza plateau. The

Egyptian Sphinx is the world's largest known monolith statue and the oldest known monumental sculpture. Construction is theorized to take place around 2,500 BCE, during the reign of pharaoh Khafra. A distinct correlation between the Giza pyramids, Sphinx and Nile river is believed by archaeoastronomists to align with the constellations Leo, Orion and the Milky Way. Another mystery refers to the Sphinx's paw structure where ground penetrating radar discovered a hollow area large enough to be a cache site. The area remains unexplored due to the water table and current theories suggest invaluable items or a tomb might be hidden inside.

Aztalan Effigy Mounds

The mysterious ancient Indian settlement located in Aztalan Wisconsin, dating to around 1,300 CE reminds archeology of how complex and strange history can be. Some researchers believe a Mississippian culture once lived here before abandoning the site due to lack of resources, by examining artifacts discovered on site. However, no written language or legends of Aztalan have been passed down throughout the ages to give us a better understanding of who they really were. According to local history, farmers plowed over the land for years before its discovery.

One of the most striking facts about visiting Aztalan is how much the effigy mounds resemble step pyramid construction, though it's important to note stone steps seen in the image were later added during site restoration. Even the site's discoverer, Timothy Johnson mistook the site for having an Aztec influence. These flat top mounds are said to be part of ceremonial practices, possibly even to house a sacred fire at each end of the settlement. Located on the Crawfish river bank, Aztalan once was a heavily fortified area with what appeared to be wood stockade walls and several watchtowers surrounding the area. The stockades appear to be related to a Mississippian site near St. Louis, called Cahokia. In the early 1950's survey work helped establish the stockade path which was later rebuilt using discarded telephone poles.

Several effigy and burial mounds are located this general area of Wisconsin, ranging in size and shape, dotting the kettle moraine. One of these mounds stands apart from the rest and is considered to be possibly the strangest mystery of the Aztalan fort. Deemed the Princess Burial, human remains were discovered with nearly 2,000 clam shell beads, some of which came from as far away as the Gulf Coast.

It gets stranger, though. In the same area, not far from the main fortification, remains with distinct characteristics of an ancient Woodland Culture were discovered near Lake Delavan and Lake Mills.

The skeletons here appear to be giant-like humans with some reported as tall as 10 feet with equally proportionate bone girth. Some believe these skeletons are proof of giants described by ancient cultures and in the Bible, though conclusive proof has yet to be placed on the table. Anthropologists argue the remains may have appeared to be giants due to soil shifting and settling which causes the bones to spread apart slowly over time.

Machu Picchu

Construction at Machu Picchu started around 1,400 CE, and was abandoned during the Spanish conquests. The location remained secret to our knowledge until modern discovery in 1911. The entire site is built in mountains which the Inca hold scared, a practice called Sacred Geography by Johan Reinhard. Around 140 structures were built using a technique the Inca mastered called ashlar, or mortar-less brick building. Stone alignments are detailed in ways to help prevent the structures from collapsing during an earthquake. Some of the stones were left with knobs which are normally removed after positioning. Evidence of how the Inca moved the much larger and heavier blocks weighing twenty to fifty tons up hill remains a mystery.

Throughout Machu Picchu we find intricately carved ritual stones called Intihuatana. Theorists describe the stones as an astronomical clock, marking the obliquity of the ecliptic, while the northern hemisphere is inclined toward the sun. The Intihuatana line up specifically to ensure no shadow is cast on March 21st and September 21st, the two dates marking the obliquity.

Mayans & Palenque

Only a very small amount of the Mayan city of Palenque is estimated to be uncovered, leaving much speculation over certain aspects in Mayan history. Theories suggest Palenque was a priestly center, arranged in an amphitheater style with one central pyramid. Among the percentage of uncovered Palenque ruins is the Palace, the Tomb of Pakal, Temples of Inscriptions, Skull XII, Lion, Sun, Cross and Foliate Cross. An aqueduct system once redirected flow of the Otulum River throughout Palenque. Over 1,500 ruins are estimated to still be buried in the Palenque city area alone.

Mayan culture is renown for celestial

influence, mathematics, ingenuity, and of course, wonderfully large constructions filled with intricate glyph carvings detailing history, beliefs, and legends. Adding to complex Mayan building practices are discoveries which reveal how many of the structures are aligned to astronomical events and key celestial configurations.

The Mayan Calendar exemplifies an impact of cosmology on their culture. Recently the calendar has sparked a substantial amount speculation due to a 5,000 year cycle projected to end on December 21st, 2012. Only one unique structure in the Palace area is unmistakably an astronomical observatory. In demonstration of Mayan architectural ability and sophisticated celestial knowledge, this four story tower lines the setting sun of the winter solstice to the center of the Temple of Inscriptions. The entire city of Chichen Itza is aligned precise to the points on a compass. Furthermore, the Pyramid of Kukulkan creates the illusion of a snake processing down the pyramid in the direction of a Cenote during the days of both autumn and spring equinoxes. Cenotes were sacred to Mayans as a principal water source and sometimes used for sacrificial offerings.

Five percent of all known Mayan structures are thought to be uncovered. A potentially rich treasure trove of Mayan history and knowledge may still exist. In 1927, Mitchell Hedges' daughter

Anna discovered a quartz crystal skull at the top of a ruined temple in the ancient Mayan city of Lubaantum, now known as Belize. After 43 years in the possession of the Hedges family, the perplexing skull was extensively examined and tested at a Hewlett Packard lab in California. Findings under a microscope demonstrated how no metal tools were used in the creation of the skull due to a distinct absence of tool markings altogether.

Analysis determined a specific gravity of 2.65 with a Mohs hardness factor of seven. Meaning that even modern tools would prove difficult to scratch or mark the crystal at all. Estimations claim a water and silicon-crystal sand process with hand-polishing for over 300 years of continuous labor could possibly achieve this result. These interesting aspects of the skull question what exactly is known of Mayan technology and prove beyond a doubt to not be a modern fabrication of any kind.

Tubes found in the zygomatic bones are precisely separated from the skull and use optical principals to channel light from the skull's base to the eye sockets. There are several light tunnels and transfers which seem to create different prismatic effects based on light sources applied to the skull from different angles. Since the Hedges discovery, two more Mayan crystal skulls were discovered in Guatemala and Mexico and brought to the United

States in 1979 by a Mayan priest. Hewlett Packard labs also tested these skulls to find nearly identical properties as the Mitchell Hedges' skull.

If the remaining 95% of Mayan civilization is truly buried, Mayan culture may considered the Egypt of the Americas. It continues to defy the modern world's perception of ancient civilizations. Given the scope of knowledge already uncovered, it is very possible we might one day rediscover forgotten technologies for the benefit of mankind.

Tiahuanaco Puma Punku

Found at the Puma Punku site in Tiahuanaco are the ruins of a massive temple complex including many hewn stone structures with extremely intricate mathematical-based carvings. Some of the stone edges are still sharp enough to cut. The process is not known how these megalithic stones were shaped and the joints are so precise that paper will not slide between the stones.

A large number of the stones are interchangeable and designed to fit into each other to provide a level surface. Carbon dating of the oldest layer of soil below the ruins estimates Puma Punku, or Door of the Cougar, construction between 530 and 600 CE. Debates continue over the designs and methods purposed to move the gigantic blocks with some weighing upward of 100 tons.

Lake Titicaca

Evidence suggests Lake Titicaca was once a saltwater sea by shores filled with fossilized seashells, and the seahorses inhabiting the water today. Now 10,000 ft. above sea level, one of Titicaca's largest islands is Isla del Sol, or Island of the Sun. The Inca believed this island is where the Sun God was born and placed many offerings here for approval, similar to the legend of El Dorado. Over 180 ruins dating to the 15th surround the lake among steep agricultural terraces.

Aramu Muru

Located only a few miles away from Titicaca is Aramu Muru's Portal, found in the Valley of the Spirits. Essentially, it is a doorway-shaped carving in the middle of rocky outcrop which in itself appears to have been molded into shape. Local legends suggest people have vanished through the stone doorway.

Tulum, City of Dawn

On the east coast of Mexico's Yucatán peninsula resides the great and mysterious ancient Mayan outpost of Tulum, formally known as Zama. From early in the 13th century to the mid 1500's, goods from inland were transported here and traded with those arriving by sea. Modern theories suggest a prominent central structure, the Castillo, acted as a lighthouse beacon to direct canoes and ships to safety past a potentially dangerous coral reef just off-shore.

Two windows in the Castillo face the sea, one is perfectly square, the other a vertical rectangle. During sunset to the west, these windows light up one at a time depending on a traveler's location near the reef. Fires lit inside the windows may take place of the sun at night, then during the day time it's possible to see a person or colored fabric from a distance on the Caribbean sea. The Castillo once utilized as a lighthouse is one plausible explanation as to its purpose, but perhaps it was also utilized for other, more divine scenarios.

At least 60 Mayan structures can be found throughout the ancient city which is fortified by three walls, two watchtowers, and a 12 meter Caribbean Sea cliff-side. Among the structures we find Temples of the Wind (Templo Dios del

Viento), Diving god (Templo del Dios Descendente), of the Frescoes, and Initial Series. Houses of the Platforms, Halach Uinik, Columns, Chultun, and of the Cenote. Then as mentioned before, El Castillo built using unique elements of traditional Mayan step pyramid architecture.

Researchers believe Tulum is a very important site in Mayan history for the worship of the Descending god Kukulcan, otherwise known as the Feathered Serpent, Quetzalcoatl to the Aztecs. According to Joseph Smith, Zama is also known as the City of Zion. He claimed this before any modern excavations of the site, during a period when Tulum could only be seen peaking out of the tops of palm trees. Artwork reliefs and symbols throughout depict scenarios closely resembling those found in the Paris Codex - and also in the Bible. Some of the paintings in particular appear to tell the story of death and resurrection of Jesus. Another unanswered mystery about Tulum is the presence of ancient stele, one dating to around 564 CE, nearly 700 years before construction began on the fort. Two theories give ideas to how this might be possible logically, either the stele was brought later or the city was rebuilt on several occasions up until its abandonment during Spanish invasions.

Teotihuacan

Left abandoned in 700 CE, Teotihuacan translates to the City of the Gods, or When Men Become Gods in Nahuatl. The city's layout is a precise scale model of the Milkyway including Pluto, Neptune, and Uranus as discovered by Hugh Harleston Jr. The three planets were not rediscovered by telescopes until the late 18th century. Three pyramids make the basis for the city. The Pyramids of the Sun, Moon, and of the Feather Serpent, all of which strikingly resemble the same configuration found in Giza, in precise celestial alignment with Orion.

Gigantic highly polished mirrors were discovered under the center of the Sun Pyramid accessible from a natural cave. Sheets of mica were found in the upper levels. Another intriguing find is at the 4th temple, deemed the Mica Temple. Large sheets of mica up to 90ft. long were found below a stone slab floor which appeared to be functional and not for decoration. Sources traced both Teotihuacan and Olmec mica to originate from over 2,000 miles away in Brazil.

Olmec Heartland

Perhaps best known for their incredibly detailed figure artworks, as defining their culture, the Mesoamerican Olmec flourished around 1400 BCE near the Bay of Campeche off the Gulf of Mexico. In addition to building large thrones and monuments, the Olmec carved colossal sized heads weighing up to fifty tons and transported them nearly sixty-two miles to the Olmec heartland. Amazingly, three of six artifacts found in the heartland give the impression that the Long Count calendar may have originated from the Olmec before the Mayans. Records indicate in 800 BCE, the Great Pyramid of La Venta was built oriented precisely 8 degrees Northwest, and 500 years later, the entire Olmec civilization vanished without any hint to where they went and why.

Gozo Malta

Two megalithic structures found on Gozo, the second largest Maltese island, called the Ggantija Temples, date to around 3,000-3,600BCE. Both temples are dedicated to the goddess of fertility. The legend describes a giant named Sunsuna who built the temple walls in one day and one night while nursing a baby. Several very large stone blocks were used in the construction. The doorway slabs feature round holes similar to offering holes found in the floors.

Numerous stone spheres were discovered on site with indications suggesting they may have been involved in moving the megaliths.

Diquis River Delta

Along the Diquis River delta in Costa Rica are hundreds of granite spheres ranging from the size of a grapefruit to the size of a person. Theories place the spheres in a rather large date window from 1,400 to 4,000 years ago. The majority of these perfectly shaped granite spheres weigh up to 16 tons with a diameter over two meters. Since no tools were found near any of the spheres, science determined their creation is due to natural process. Calculations for some of the spheres demonstrate a 0.2% error rate or less, highly suggesting some sort of human intervention. Since the 1930s discovery in Costa Rica, world attention helped discover hundreds of other sphere formations in other countries. Though not proven, many of the stone spheres around the world are thought to be carved.

Carnac

Truly one of the most puzzling megalithic sites in the world is a very large field containing over 3,000 megaliths weighing between 20 to 350 tons each, outside of the French village of Carnac. Carbon dating places some stones to be as old as 4,500 BCE during the Neolithic period. The stones are arranged in different alignments, some of which accurately display mathematical concepts such as Pythagorean Theorem thousands of years before documented by Pythagoras. Among the rows of megaliths are very large Dolmen structures consisting of a large capstone resting on several pillars. One of the most famous examples is the Dolmen of Crucno found at Breton Village, with a forty ton capstone resting on nine pillars.

Coral Castle

With a 20th century anything is possible vision, Ed Leedskalnin created a masterpiece coral stone sculpture garden in the 1930s by himself that defies explanation. A single, five foot tall, 100 lb. man was able to hang a nine ton gate which pivots effortlessly with a single touch, inviting guests into a rock garden of amazement.

Included in the wonders is a thirty ton Polaris aligned telescope as part of the 150 ton North Wall and Throne Room, fully functional coral stone rocking chairs, 2.5 ton heart-shaped table, a single piece stone spiral staircase, and a three ton functional turnstile. Estimates claim Ed quarried over 1,100 tons of coral rock in order to build the gardens.

Mystery has engulfed the area with questions attempting to figured out how he managed to build so largely, completely alone, and with such precision; something that undoubtedly would be attributed to an entire ancient civilization. Ed is most famous for the stone undercut, a precise cut under the quarried stones which has not been explained by modern masons.

There are witnesses who believed they caught Ed moving these blocks through the air and Ed once wrote how he discovered the way in which the Egyptians built. So far, modern science has not deciphered Ed's methods and remains baffled. Some theorists speculate he discovered a way to use the Geomagnetic grid to generate anti-gravity waves. Examination of Ed's tools started inside his tool room. Found within are many different types of pulley and hoist systems as well as devices which look like electric motor parts. The wire-wrapped bottles are very interesting as they demonstrate very large resistors using a glass core instead of ceramic. Evidently, Mr. Leedskalnin experimented with electricity and methods of moving very heavy stones.

In the recording at the start of the tour, Ed claims a three year duration to move the castle from locations, contrary to the idea of an over night miracle. He also confirms in the recording, dates which are carved on the Obelisk piece: Made 1928, Moved 1932, Born 1887, Latvia. During a tour we had a special experience of our own, closely followed by a curious Red Headed Rock Agama lizard. He would peak at us through some of the rocks and appeared quite a few times when least expected. A few of the photos and some video footage features our pleasant friend. At times it did seem as though the Agama might be carrying Ed's spirit.

Oak Island

A very ingenious theorized treasure trap is on Oak Island, off the coast of Halifax, Canada. In 1795 a teenager found what appeared to be an underground shaft which later revealed alternating layers of foreign flagstone and timber. As excavations took place, after a certain depth, the shaft would fill with water preventing the workers from continuing further. After several failed attempts it was discovered the core shaft had feeder tunnels stretching to the ocean, deliberately flooding the area once one of the tunnels were hit.

Experiments with red dye traced three connected tunnels and hinted at the possibility of more further down. With obvious evidence of a type of hydraulic protection system and several strange markings found on stones around the island, many theories of what lies below have spawned. Trace element testing displays higher than normal concentrations of mercury and radiation in some areas. One mysterious discovery came from a small camera maneuvered down a tunnel. The camera caught a glimpse of what appeared to be tools, some which look ancient and others with futuristic look beyond our time.

Bosnian Pyramid Complex

Located in the Visoko Valley, the Bosnian Pyramid Complex is known as the first pyramid discovered in Europe. Ruins of a medieval town, believed to be the site of Bosnian king Tvtko of Kotromanic, were found on the flat top along with an entrance to the complex. Throughout the site, large structures have been identified as pyramids of Sun, Moon, Dragon, Love, and the Temple of Earth, due to distinct similarities to the pyramid complex of Teotihuacan.

According to a geological team report conducted by the Federation of Bosnia and

Herzegovina Association of Geologists, the Bosnian Pyramids are estimated to date to 32,000 BCE which significantly out-dates Egyptian pyramids by approximately 27,000 years.

The find rocked the geological world. Scientists across the globe accept the geological dates on the basis the Bosnian Pyramids were actually formed naturally. Formations like this sometimes referred to be flatirons which are found all over the world. Despite evidence leaning toward natural processes, building evidence and discoveries are beginning to point the pyramid to be entirely man-made.

Massive underground tunnel systems unearthed at the site reveal an intricate system connecting the pyramids. Each branch of the tunnels is ventilated every 30 meters and contains sandstone monoliths engraved with symbols of an ancient writing system. The tunnels were once used by the Yugoslavian army during the period of communism, similar to those used in Croatia. Large parts of the tunnel system needed to be excavated and scientists can only pinpoint up to ten meters of tunnel actually used by the Yugoslav army. Recently, about one mile away from the Bosnian Pyramids, scientists found a very large sign composed of six letters similar to ancient writings found inside the tunnel systems. Each letter is approximately one mile long and nearly 800 meters wide and the meaning is up for debate.

Coupled with the Bosnian Pyramid controversy, 20 spherical stone balls similar to those found in Costa Rica are located across the Bosnia region including a one meter diameter ball cut completely in half. The spheres are made from granite and not finely polished like their Costa Rican counterparts. Several smaller holes scatter their surfaces which lead scientists to believe they were most likely formed by natural processes like the shaping of rocks by water over long periods of time. The actual amount of granite spheres located throughout Bosnia is debatable. Current discoveries claim the spheres to be nothing more than accidental finds during pyramid excavations.

Racetrack Playa & Death Valley

Research conducted at the Racetrack Playa area in Death Valley by both NASA and students of Slipperyrock University has lead to interesting conclusions over the phenomena of moving rocks. NASA claims the rocks are most likely moved by strong wind gusts, calculating that at least 150 mph would be necessary to move the largest of the rocks tipping scales at nearly 700 pounds. Students of Slipperyrock determined a slope does exist but they feel it is far too insignificant to affect the movement of the rocks. They also gathered radiation and magnetic anomaly data during the process of cause elimination.

Data presented by NASA and Slipperyrock students does not encompass the entire dynamic system at work in the Death Valley region. In reference to NASA's wind theory and pictured rocks which are proportionately more vertical than girth; High wind forces against those sail-like rocks would logically cause them to tumble along the flats yet the transient path is smooth, consistent, and highly accurate to the rock traveling along a single face. In reference to the students of Slipperyrock and the slope discovery; This is on the right track, almost literally. Even-though the slope may appear to be minuscule and insignificant enough to move large rocks, its a positive indicator to the processes happening below the flats. Slope findings dismiss the possibility of an optical illusion whereby the surrounding area tricks the viewer into thinking the area is level or sloping in a different direction.

New-age theory suggests Death Valley and Racetrack Playa are part of a super-dynamic tectonic system influenced by deep area seismic activity. The entire flat plain fluctuates in a double sea-saw type motion. Transients demonstrate the path relative to activity which previously took place below the surface. Like a dynamic bellows, pressure placed on one end of the plain causes another end to rise or tilt respectively. In this case the pressures are applied below ground, forcing parts of the crust to inflate and retract.

Recent slope measurements demonstrate the rocks seem to be moving in a very slow upward incline indicating the system's fluctuation has since changed. One visualization is thinking of the flat plain as an upside-down trampoline. When pressure excites one section of the trampoline, the object at the pressure point is forced away, similar to the rocks at Racetrack Playa. Tension differential, though, is why the rocks do not jump from one place to the next. Instead, the rocks slide along as different tethers which push upward and then relax. This is why in certain areas large groups of rocks seem to move together while others nearby don't.

Areas moving together are affected by the same tether. The entire system is composed of several independent tethers relative to the activity below. Essentially, by tectonic process in a linear fashion, pushing on one side of the valley creates enough tension to bulge areas of the surface until the opposite side shifts ever to slightly, releasing the pressure and removing the bulges.

Another concept explaining the mysterious moving rocks of Death Valley suggests the rapid freezing and thawing of moisture on the surface is responsible for moving rocks in short periods of time. Temperatures in the desert at night dip low enough to freeze, which may encase the rocks or create an optimal surface tension allowing them to slide easily.

Angel Oak Tree

Protected in a public park on John's Island in South Carolina, the Angel Oak tree is definitely a most impressive living site to visit. One may experience an unexplainable feeling of calmness and peace as they walk under the huge 17,000 square ft. shade canopy while gazing in amazement. It truly feels like a connection to nature and the past. With an estimated age close to 1,400 years old, the ancient Angel Oak tree, named after Martha and Justus Angel, has witnessed a lot of history, survived the logging industry, and even a hurricane.

The trunk alone measures 25-1/2 ft. and some of the limbs are so large that they've begun to grow upward after crawling along the ground. Damage over the years resulted in many branches needing reinforcing with wiring and supports for preservation. Angel Oak's mesmerizing experience will hopefully continue on for many years to come and allow many more people to see the living beauty first hand.

Time & Space

Crop Circles

Along with UFO sightings, crop circle formations date back in history have since gained public popularity during the 20th century. The earliest known circle reports come from an 815CE account by archbishop of Lyon demanding ransom on behalf of the Magonians for flattening crops. Lyon also banned pagans from taking seeds from crop circle formations for fertility rituals.

Years later we find a 1678CE woodcut showing the devil mowing a field into patterns. Apparently the farmer refused to pay the cutting fee and swore to have the devil do it instead. Early 12th century accounts of circle formations were known as fairy rings which are a naturally forming phenomenon of fungus growing in circular shapes. Fairy rings might be the answer for a few, very primitive simple crop circle formations. Fungus does not seem to answer many complex designs witnessed today.

Hoaxers have stepped forward and claimed to to be the creators of the more intricate designs using a board and ropes overnight. They were put to the test with live sessions, given a formation drawing and asked to replicate it as accurate as possible. With credit due, they did obtain a very close rendition, but they were not able to obtain the level of precision found in other complex designs. Many remaining formations cannot be explained by conventional means or logic. One famous example is the overnight Milk Hill circle in Wiltshire, a composition of 409 circles fit into a perfect spiral formation 244 meters in diameter.

Research into crop circle formation, composition, and mathematics reveals levels of precision and engineering currently unknown in the scientific field. Certain fields provide biological evidence supporting changes in soil composition. Alterations to the DNA were discovered in some crop circle affected plant materials. There are fields providing physical evidence in the form of tiny, nearly microscopic iron shavings scattered throughout the soil and embedded into parts of the crop.

With over 10,000 reported formations its understandable to have several fields reported to show no change in biological makeup of the crops and soil affected. Organizations like the International Crop Circle Database are working to catalog circle formations with reports dating back to the 1940s, in an effort to decipher the phenomenon.

Genuine crop circle appearances, those believed not to have originated by a human, have slowly declined over the past decade. Theorists are unsure what this means in the overall picture. Perhaps the quiet time is a calm before the storm, or the original intended message is believed to have been received.

Unidentified Flying Objects

Historical evidence suggests an increase in UFO activity near the beginning and during times of war and conflict. Reports of unidentified flying objects consistently date back throughout the ages and are not a new age phenomenon.

Past civilizations describe flying objects in terms relating to their current knowledge and interpretation of the events, of the specific reported time period. One prominent case involves several hundred sightings written throughout city gazettes during the time of the Black Plague epidemic. Cases of cigar shaped flying vessels were reported, along with a mist filling the air, to the point that people believed they could see the plague coming toward them.

Another such incident refers to a single flying object reported over several countries spanning from Scotland all the way to eastern China, detailed from individual sighting reports in those respective countries. The intriguing mystery of the reports is that they all happened within the same time span. Countries at war during the period relied on courier communication of letters estimated to take far longer than any of the documented gazette accounts.

Events in the 20th century such as the Black Forest in 1936 and Roswell in 1947 acted like a rooster call to those who weren't previously aware, bringing significant attention to the possibilities of UFOs existing around the world. Both cases are filled with controversy and seem to lack empirical evidence necessary to satisfy skeptics. Virtually no evidence was reported or found regarding the Black Forest incident, but the crash is documented to have happened.

Certain beliefs claim the Nazis retrieved the wreckage and destroyed related reports. It's believed they used it for reverse engineering to help create newer technologies. This coincides with numerous reports involving balls of light, or FOO, over European skies in 1944 believed to be a German secret weapon. The theory also references how much more advanced German technology was at the time in comparison to the other countries in the world. It may also explain the culprit of the 1942 Battle of Los Angeles, when an unidentified flying craft triggered over 1,400 shells to be fired in an hour time period.

The Roswell incident was attributed to a weather balloon by Major Curtan in a telegraph sent to the FBI. Many believe that between the type of debris found at the wreckage site, reports before the crash, and inconsistencies in the military reporting procedures, it was actually a government UFO cover-up. Eye witness claims, a supposed alien autopsy, and new photo analysis of evidence continue to fuel speculations of what really happened in Roswell.

Sightings during the 1940s might also be explained by Fu-Go weapons, or Japanese balloon bombs. Around 1,000 balloons with an integrated bomb and trigger are estimated to have reached the United States and Canada by taking advantage of the global jet stream air path. The Japanese claimed more than 9,000 Fu-Go were launched with the first series in 1944 from Honshu Japan, during the same time of FOO reports over Germany. The problem with this solution is the glowing orbs over Germany could be flown through with an airplane.

Only one known case with cause of death to a Fu-Go weapon was documented in Oregon. An unsuspecting family on a picnic stumbled across a Fu-Go device in 1945, accidentally triggering it out of curiosity. According to further accounts, it is known the British were also experimenting with crude balloon-type bombs during 1942-1944 possibly contributing to the UFO sighting phenomenon at the time.

Outside of the busy skies of the 1940s, cases of UFO related incidents and sightings have risen substantially over the years. A designated organization established in 1969, once known as the Midwest UFO Network, called MUFON currently tracks and stores reports of unidentified flying object sightings across the world. Their mission is one of analytical and scientific study of UFO phenomenon in interest of the general public, for the benefit of humanity.

A single organization working to catalog, organize, and decipher report information makes a lot of sense in determining the reasons for the strange phenomenon reoccurring throughout human history. With everyone's help, it is possible to research and finally explain UFO phenomenon of the ages.

Unidentified Submersible Objects

Recently gaining momentum with popular culture are Unidentified Flying Object sightings. A well known high concentration of sightings, known as a USO hot spot, is around the island of Puerto Rico. These USO reports share common elements as UFO cases though they usually involve unknown objects submerged in water which are cresting or leaving the surface. Some believe an unidentified submersible object is the precursor to a UFO sighting. Eye-witness accounts around inhabited islands and shorelines have steadily risen over the past 50 years.

One of the most crucial sightings was reported by Columbus during the voyage to North America. The crew and himself claimed to have seen a glowing, pulsing ball of light leave from beneath the ocean's surface only to jet away into the sky. The report ends up being so astonishing that the news travels back home where Columbus is tried in court, not for seeing or reporting a USO, but for describing it to be similar to the Jewish Menorah.

Theories attempt to explain USO sightings ranging from bio-luminescent sea creatures, ball-lightning, and astronomical phenomenon, but do not seem to entirely fit case reports. USO are known to seamlessly transition from water to air without creating a splash or noticeable break in water tension. Also, the objects are sometimes witnessed at the top of a waterspout.

Though speculative, ideas about the purpose of USO and what they are doing include harvesting hydrogen-based fuel or traveling to or from an underwater base. Thousands of reported sightings from the sea, air, and land, stem from credible sources building an idea that UFO sightings correlate to USO sightings.

Rosslyn Chapel

Ernst Chladni originally documented the appearance of visual musical patterns in 1787 by vibrating a fine powder on a metal plate to frequencies of sounds. These patterns have been dubbed Cymatics by modern science. One interesting coincidence is how Ernst's discovery seems to appear in the 15th century Rosslyn Chapel.

Thomas Mitchell spent 20 years trying to decipher 215 blocks he presumed to be encoded musical cubes found along the pillars and arches inside Rosslyn Chapel. The blocks seem to show a clear understanding of Cymatics well before Chladni's time. Freemasons designed and built the chapel to include symbols of the Knights Templar, believed to be a preservation of the society's secrets. Geometry of sound dates to ancient Egyptian and Chinese cultures. It is key belief in Freemasonry's structure of life and the cosmos.

For inquiring minds, the Rosslyn Chapel musical cubes present an entirely new a sense of dimension to the Rosslyn puzzle. Along with theories of the chapel being an inter-dimensional portal, these musical cubes add to the overall complexity. Research suggests Rosslyn might be more than a temple of creative celebratory decoration.

Cymatics

Visual reference to sound vibrations is credited to German physicist and musician Ernst Chladni. Ernst used a violin bow, metal plates and sand to produce different patterns based on specific sound frequencies in 1787. His discovery proved sound affects physical matter and how the vibrations are capable of creating geometrical patterns.

Though Chladni is attributed to visually demonstrating sound's affect on matter, there are historical accounts which may prove this auditory science to exist long before his time. The Rosslyn Chapel features intricately patterned cubes theorized to be musical cubes. The ancient Egyptians and Chinese cultures mention similar practices inadvertently extending the known time-line.

American mathematician Nathaniel Bowditch and French mathematician Jules-Antoine Lissajous both spent a significant amount of time studying the results from Chladni's experiments. They determined independently that frequencies were the condition responsible for the pattern designs. Lissajous then perceives the variations in shapes are due to phase differential.

Two hundred years after Chladni's discovery, Hans Jenny published a book called Cymatics – The Structure and Dynamics of Waves and Vibrations. Ernst's experiments were reproduced in further depth using crystal oscillators and a Jenny tonoscope. With the tonoscope, a human voice can be visualized directly on the metal plates without an intermediate link.

Modern Cymatics experiments with water and liquid-based materials such as a cornstarch mixture beautifully display how sound affects physical matter. Although the science may appear as a newly discovered phenomenon, it roots deeply among a variety of civilizations and their understanding of our physical existence.

Dinosaur Appendages

Depictions of dinosaurs today may not be entirely accurate. The skeletal framework suggests a basic shape of the animal and provides enough rational for certain scientific conclusions. However, examples from animals living today such as the Sperm Whale demonstrate how animal shape doesn't always conform to the skeletal structure such as a Blue Whale.

Is it possible that some dinosaurs had a spermaceti-type organ designed for a specific water or land purpose during the period? The remains are not found because they decay similar to cartilages and flesh. Modern animal fibrous models provide a general understanding of how an ancient animal might have appeared but don't guarantee an entirely accurate reproduction.

Another key point here is how an animal's extended sensory organ decay away as well. In cases like an elephant trunk, our only clues to their existence in ancient animals seem to come from modern living descendants.   Animals discovered from dinosaur periods may actually look quite different from their commonly accepted renditions. Given the time-line between today's animal relatives and their great ancestors, it is not unreasonable to believe those ancestors might have had additional appendages or limbs which we may never know by scientific fact to have ever existed at all.

Pressure on the scientific community from the general public to produce visual reference of unearthed bone sets could have rushed the process. Artistic interpretations have shaped common beliefs to become the accepted norm. It would be very difficult are require a lot of time to determine if certain species of Dinosaurs really did have an extra apparatus, especially considering the biological decay difference between fleshy materials and bone.

Betelgeuse

Betelgeuse is a red super-giant star located in the constellation Orion between 490-780 light years from Earth. Studies indicate the star is losing mass at a rapid rate, and may be on the brink of a type II supernova. Scientific estimates place the time of supernova within the next million years, but there remains a significant issue.

Due to the distance there is a possibility that Betelgeuse may have already went supernova centuries ago and the light has yet to reach Earth. This is coupled with prophetic 2012 apocalyptic doomsday scenarios as another sign to the world's end.

Theories claim the world would have two suns for a period of time, causing up to 2 weeks of intense light before fading back to the normal day/night cycle over several months as the supernova light dwindles. According to scientific research the only known Betelgeuse emissions, other than high levels of photons, is a high concentration of neutrinos which may be of great research value to endeavors like the IceCube Neutrino Observatory in Antarctica.

Polar Shifts

When the Earth's magnetic field shifts, it's theorized that gaps may evolve in the magnetosphere as the process becomes chaotic before settling into its new position. According to geologists and other scientific research, the estimation for the last apocalyptic pole-flip, south to north, happened over 780,000 years ago. Evidence suggests a cycle of pole flips nearly every 50,000 years incidentally claiming Earth is getting closer to the 16th known polar flip since the last world devastating event.

A polar-shift does not happen over night. By calculation it is a gradual process over a period of 4,500 to 5,000 year. This does not in anyway mean that one day it's beautiful and the next day is an apocalyptic terror-storm.

References to associative 2012 polar shifts often neglect to include this significant detail as it tends to remove the punch from the apocalyptic theory. However, one common phenomena related to polar flips as suggested by Earth weather and climate models does include super storms with winds reaching the 300-400mph range. Weather changes over Europe have brought attention to the super storm scenario though a change in weather patterns doesn't necessarily mean the Earth's poles are swapping.

Face in the Mayan Calendar

A little over half a year has passed since the huge controversial hype over the Mayan calendar's supposed prediction of world annihilation on 2012's winter solstice event, and the calendar as well as the Mayans have received very little media attention since. The press wants a huge story from an old rock, and when the day passed without much of a sneeze, calendar mention went by the wayside. Multiple theories and speculations flew around social media and television channels, yet nothing we know in this physical realm changed.

One thing for certain is, many millions of people wanted to see a spectacular natural event take place in their lifetime, and that dream likely did not die off overnight for true believers.

Think of this: Let's say with some level of technology or psychic intuition we were able to predict a future event which possibly could destroy the face of our planet - Would we leave a comparable artifact for future generations to discover? An interesting thing about this concept is, it can be said almost without a doubt, no way José. The reason is because we currently know of a theoretical destructive time billions of years in the future, when the sun reaches the end of its life-cycle and grows large enough to eat the Earth whole. If we know this, why do we not leave a stone artifact to warn future generations of the event? Can we really expect an ancient civilization to have done this?

What's more, there is a face (Tonatiuh) in the middle of the Mayan calendar. To the Aztecs, Tonatiuh is a symbol of the 5th world, a sun god, and leader of heaven - To us, a reason the calendar is also known as the Sunstone. There is a new twist on Sunstone concepts, however, suggesting the 2012 date was either miscalculated or counted from the wrong starting point. What if instead of destruction, the calendar pointed to an entirely different date, say around 1844, when Joseph Smith, (José!), created multiple sun-stones in the

Nauvoo temple, Illinois only to see them fall in the face of persecution. At the time Mormonism wasn't well liked by other, more established religions, and many of his celestial inspired creations were destroyed. Could the Aztec calendar and Nauvoo temple event somehow be linked together?

Does the face in the center represent a messiah, literally the Son, and not the physical sun Earth orbits around? In an actual photo of the calendar, the face does look a little like renditions of Jesus over the years. There are certainly some characteristics it has in common, a sort of crown, locks of hair, facial expression, eye shape. Maybe that's a bit of a stretch, but for some reason the calendar gives an entirely different meaning if Tonatiuh represents the messiah.

Environmental Phenomena

Throughout the ages weather conditions account for many strange phenomena. Due to the complexity behind these strange happenings, it's only suiting to have long investigations and mounds of intricate data necessary for explanation. Since most of the research does not directly involve eye-witness accounts from the event, scientists base theories on the resulting evidence. Strange weather related phenomena found in this section is rigorously studied by many scholars before any acceptable conclusions are reached.

Star Jelly

An English Latin dictionary dating to 1440CE is the first known written account of a substance referred to as Star Jelly, a gelatinous material discovered randomly on Earth's surface. Folklore at the time suggested the slime was remnant of falling or shooting stars as no other explanation could be determined. Modern science presented several new theories including animal byproduct, a type of algae, and even a dry material that becomes jelly-like when moisture is introduced. In fact, a similar process is used in NASA space experiments. Dried microbes were put into suspended animation and then sprinkled with a bit of water to bring them back to life.

There are known microbes capable of being exposed to the vacuum of space directly in the suspended state and then be brought back to life with water in the lab. With star jelly though, testing done on a selection of specimens has yet to reveal any DNA material, furthering claims that it's not a living organism. The jelly is a clue to what is possible in this Universe. If science discovers Star Jelly to be an Earth-bound deposit from a meteor, the origin of life might be elsewhere.

Strange Rainfall

For many years people have witnessed very odd and strange types of rainfall, slightly altering the perception of what reality might be. Aquatic animals such as fish and frogs are known to blanket landscapes in large quantities. Further accounts talk of large amounts of dried plant matter, flesh type material, and blood. The most common sensible explanation for odd rain involves a weather system with high winds such as a tornado or waterspout sucking up a shallow body of water, animals and all, into the sky and ejecting the contents several miles away from the site. Blood rain reports are identified to occur in areas (for the most part) where colored dust or fine organic material is absorbed by water which then condenses and falls in another location. The red rain in Kerala, for example, was discovered to be very similar to algae and fungal spores found in the area.

Ball Lightning & Vitrification

Also known as plasma balls, reports of ball lightning have trickled in over the years. Accounts describe a sphere-shaped bright object streaking horizontally across the sky and can range from a quiet vanish to a very loud explosion.

The vitrification process requires very high temperatures to turn outer layers of rock and sand into a smooth glass. Areas of vitrified desert are explained to be the result of a meteor explosion over the area, creating intense heat in the process. A similar result was achieved during the detonation of the atomic bomb, demonstrating an idea of the type of power required to vitrify parts of the Earth's crust.

Forts in Scotland, France, and Turkey clearly show evidence of vitrification, but the answers to how remains in question. Estimations suggest that for these forts to reach vitrification by human involvement, temperatures in excess of 1,000 degrees Celsius are necessary. Theories claim the forts were deliberately used as large kilns in order to strengthen them from attackers.

The process would be long, tedious, and very impractical. Other theories suggest these forts might be victims of an ancient atomic war.

Vitrification is a phenomenon evident in deserts around the world, often believed to result from an intense blast of heat capable of melting sand and rocks to create glass-infused crust. Usually these types of blasts are attributed to meteor explosions just above the Earth's surface, given the right circumstances, although any such blast has not been observed first-hand.

We also know vitrified glass can be the result of lightning striking sandy areas to create fulgurite root-shaped tube deposits of fused silica quartz, a very different looking vitrification when compared to vast areas encrusted in layers of glass. Some researchers now believe large areas of desert glass may be connected with ancient bomb testing or wars, and that the invention of the atomic bomb might have happened well before the modern age.

There are references to nuclear type events in ancient texts such as the Mahabharata, describing large explosive events with similar precision to how the modern age would describe a nuclear event. Billowing smoke clouds, shock-waves, flames, and vitrified glass surfaces. However, these melted glass surfaces don't stop in the desert. They've also been discovered in ancient cities such as Catal Huyukin, in the Province of Piaui, forts in England, Babylonia, Death Valley, Arabia, Gobi, Mohave Desert, Norway, Canary Islands, and the list goes on without sufficient scientific explanation in most cases.

A handful of researchers believe the ancient Scottish, English and Irish forts were possibly intentionally vitrified as a means of strengthening the fortifications, but they find problems with feasibility and resource allocation to achieve this type of castle defense. There are also quite a few solid stone structures similar to the forts that appear to be melted in some way with no reasonable scientific explanation. Pointing toward ancient atomic war does explain certain results such as glass crusting, but unfortunately there is not enough tangible evidence to support these claims. Even if, remotely, the vitrified forts and deserts were byproducts of meteor explosions in our atmosphere, why have they never been witnessed and why do we not have historical accounts of this but instead of mass destruction type events?

Geographic Mapping

Ancient mysterious locations of peak interest can be connected along the same belt, around the world between 20° and 32° north latitude. The belt also connects the Bermuda triangle with the Dragon's triangle, two epicenters for anomalies and geomagnetic fluctuations according to some theorists. One significant location along the line is Mexico's Zone of Silence. The area is considered to be a dead-zone where radio and electronic equipment do not function. There are accounts of this site in particular being capable of attracting meteors and other flying objects.

Why is there a great number of key sites located along the same line around the world? Some conclude it's a mere coincidence or attribute the locations to environmental conditions such as longer and warmer days allowing for the building of larger, more complicated structures. One such theory suggests the spiritual connection of Earth is held together inside by a tetrahedron of energy and the pyramids are located at the points where the tetrahedron meets with the Earth's surface. This could explain exactly why the pyramids around Earth are located in their exact positions, as a way to amplify and/or harness the spiritual energies of the planet.

The tetrahedron is a closed isometric crystal form and utilized in Crystal field theory as the second most common complex where four molecules form a tetrahedron around a metal ion. This theory is sometimes used to account for magnetic properties of transition metal complexes. In other words, the tetrahedral symmetry of the Earth's magnetic field might account for pyramid location around the world. Geomagnetic anomalies like the Sedona Vortex, the Bermuda Triangle and Devil's Triangle spark further research in attempt to discover why these areas across the globe behave the way they do. An evolved field of science called Tectonomagnetism, for example, is a method of monitoring changes in the Earth's tectonic plates and how those changes relate to Earth's geomagnetic field.

Voynich Manuscript

Composed of 240 vellum pages written in an undecipherable language, the Voynich Manuscript is quite perplexing and continues to intrigue theorists since its public release over 40 years ago. Confusion over the Voynich Manuscript created several theories purposed by scientists of different disciplines. To some, the medieval script resembles an East or Central Asia language in raw form, which is almost instantly noticeable by looking at similarities in symbolism.

Historic record provides an indication that the language was invented for the purpose of the book or a series of related texts. Several explorers from East Asia were known to invent alphabets to protect their discoveries. For this reason some suggest the book is a cipher with symbols introduced into hide information. Interestingly, the manuscript carbon dates (by vellum) to roughly between 1400 and 1440, not too long before ciphers were gaining popularity in Europe. There are at least ten major theories with scientific merit to what the manuscript might be. An actual translation remains unknown.

Aside from the strange language found throughout the script, there are illustrations adding to the mystery. The drawings are believed to section the book into six parts: Herbalism, Astronomy, Biology, Cosmology, Pharmacology, and Recipes. Interpretation of the drawings appear to be Herbal related and demonstrate plant combinations, or hybrids with the leaves of one plant mixed with the roots and flowers from another. A theory by William Newbold states the circular shaped drawings look like cross-sections of the plants which could only be witnessed by looking at them with a microscope. Although his theory was dismissed for speculation, looking at the drawings for a brief moment could easily give one the idea they might be cross-sectional diagrams.

Controversy surrounding the Voynich Manuscript resulted in accusations and claims the book is a hoax. This is based solely on a statement, if there is no decipherable information there must be no information at all. By far the strongest evidence the medieval script is not a hoax, at least by modern times, is the vellum's carbon date result.

The script is considered too sophisticated when compared to other hoaxes during the same period. Interpretation of the illustrations alone provide insight and clues toward understanding the text written alongside. Painting the overall picture that the Voynich is possibly as a guide to plants, herbal remedies, and their cycles with close relation to the stars. The concept is not unreasonable to hunter-gatherers, and it's repeated on countless occasions throughout history. Of course, there is the possibility the script may translate to something divine in purpose, relating the heavens above to the Earth.

It's extremely selfish to think we are the only existing intelligent living beings in the Universe.

Mystics

Fountain of Youth

There are a great number of stories about the legendary Fountain of Youth. A mystical spring which grants eternal life to those who drink from it, allowing people to live forever. One of the earliest known mentions dates to around 450 BC when Herodotus, a Greek historian, wrote about finding the water of life in Ethiopia. Spanish explorer Juan Ponce de León, heard of the Fountain of Youth from the people of Puerto Rico, believed the story, and set search to find it. He was not associated with the legend until after his death in 1521. The fountain is rumored to be located in the land he named Florida. Despite efforts, the Fountain of Youth has not been found to this date.

Shangri' La

James Hilton wrote of a mystical place called Shangri' La in his 1933 book, the Lost Horizon. Described as a hidden Utopian paradise, Shangri' La is an untouched world secretly located on Earth, away from the tainted common bustle of society. People who are fortunate to live in the harmony of the Himalayan Dream age very slowly and are forever happy with everything they could ever need and aspire to. The 1973 movie version of the book depicts a long and treacherous journey to find this hidden paradise on Earth. The High Lama's time could not last forever and his lessons give hope that one day we may all find our own Shangri La somewhere along the journey of life.

Ancient Weapons in Mythology

Euhemerism is a theory named after a 320 BCE mythologist named Euhemerus who claimed that myths are really a distorted reality of past events believed to have taken place. Through the years, they become stretched similar to a tall-tale fish story. Some theorists believe myths are over-glorified accounts of a person who made such a profound impact on their culture, their story would live on throughout the ages for all to know.

Myths often involve supernatural events or objects unfathomable to exist even to this day. Although many of the stories and fables are just that, it's interesting to purpose the idea of Euhemerism relating to the incredible weapons and armor at the disposal of ancient mythological stars. One reason why this topic is surfacing in the modern world might be due to amazing leaps in technology over the last hundred years.

Arguably one of the most famous Greek Olympians, is Zeus. Known to the Romans as Jupiter, the God of Thunder carries a thunderbolt capable of destroying entire cities in a single throw. Similarly, the Lord of Heaven and mountain god, Indra, is known in Hindu mythology for his thunderbolt weapon called the Vajra. Interestingly enough there is a twist. Kongo is the Vajra equivalent name in Japanese, but for the trident-shaped lightning staff which belonged to Koya-no-Myoin, a Japanese mountain god. Three cultures share the concept of an ancient weapon known as the thunderbolt, capable of mass destruction.

As the Kongo emits a bright light to give man wisdom and insight, its power transcends cultures once again, to the Norse god Thor. His destructive hammer, called Mjollnir, symbolizes lightning too. Thor required iron gloves and a belt of strength to wield Mjollnir. Modern day science tells us iron gloves would probably conduct electricity instead of projecting it outward. There is a possibility the gloves indicate why his hammer would return after it was thrown. The exact type of technology swims in unknown waters for now. Maybe there is more to Thor's story that wasn't passed down or was left out intentionally, perhaps not considered crucial to the overall moral.

In perception of those who passed stories down through the generations, mythological weapons of destruction distinctly demonstrate the sheer power of the gods on several levels. Poseidon, known to the Romans as Neptune, the Lord of the Sea carries a trident similar in description to the Kongo, but with powers closely related to the sea instead of the clouds above. His trident is believed to shake the earth, shatter objects, and manifest both horses and water spouts. This power resembles current sought after technologies in forms of weather manipulation, and is coincidentally reminiscent of late Tesla research.

Nikola claimed to create an oscillating device designed to tune into structural frequencies, causing those objects to break apart from the vibrations. Witness reports near Tesla experiments talk of the ground and buildings shaking though nothing was proved beyond a doubt as the work of Tesla. Other weapons mentioned in ancient mythologies could really exist to this day, lending creditability to the Euhemerism theory.

The Norse god Odin and his spear called Grungir is known to never miss a mark. This eerily resembles modern missile technologies using pin-point lasers or heat guided radar to hit targets without failure. Odin's bow can shoot 10 arrows every pull, and might be considered an ancient description of modern rapid fire weapons. Even Odin's sword, capable of cutting an anvil in two, is not a far-fetched idea. Apollo's far-shooting silver bow might be considered a weapon of the missile launching type except for one issue. His bow could also heal, something which modern weapons are not designed to do. The stories of the poisoned arrows of Heracles, known as Hercules in Roman, and Ysbaddadan's venomous spears, present the idea of applying chemicals to weapons to enhance their destructive powers.

Some mythological accounts blatantly describe weapons of mass destruction on a monumental scale, the size of an atom or nuclear bomb. Hindu mythology discusses the Brahmastra. When discharged it creates devastating environmental damage, rendering the land barren in the (fall out) area, where life ceases to exist at ground zero. It causes men and women to become unable to reproduce while decreasing rainfall to the point of drought.

The Pashupatastra shares a similar account except as a device capable of vanquishing all beings, which can be triggered by the mind, eyes, words, or a bow. Then there is the Biblical mention of the Ark of the Covenant. A mysterious box used in conjunction with ram horn trumpets to bring down the walls of Jericho. History references people getting sick or dying from touching the Ark, along with many warnings not to touch or look at it. Although these mythologies might lend merit by Euhemerism theory, science does not have distinguished proof to differentiate these stories from ancient descriptions of factual events.

The Emerald Tablet

Imagine a concept, that if Newton's dedication to the Emerald Tablet instead followed a different path outside the realm of alchemy and delved more into spirituality and its relationship between mankind and the world around us. As many scholars throughout the ages, Newton became obsessed with an idea that any element could be transmuted into any other element at the hands of alchemy, but the philosopher's stone quickly turned itself into a fantasy goose chase after discovering the shear level of complexity involved;

Could a man ever possess the power Midas created in a chemistry lab? The following is a literal interpretation of the Emerald Tablet of Hermes, and an alternative possibility of what his mysterious ancient text could be trying to tell us. The tablet begins with:

Truly without deceit, certain, and most
veritable. That which is below
corresponds to that which is above; And
that which is above corresponds to that
which is below.

Purity. Either in the sense of a pure element, or for a soul to reach enlightenment, to be accepted into the heavens, and into an afterlife free from evil. As a herald, Hermes guided souls of the dead to the underworld and was also believed to bring dreams to mortals at night. It is possible these lines refer to a relationship of souls between the living and the dead. Those in the underworld were once above, and those above will in time be in the underworld.

To accomplish the miracles of the one
thing; And just as all things come from
this one thing; Through the meditation of
one mind; So do all created things
originate from this one thing; Through
transformation.

Perhaps here is where Newton first noticed clues the Emerald tablet could be a secret reference, leading eventually to the conclusion of a hidden alchemical practice used to create the philosopher's stone.

Literally the verse says everything comes from one and by means of transformation, but it's the line regarding meditation of one mind suggesting a more spiritual significance.

> *Its father is the sun;*
> *Its mother is the moon*
> *The wind carries it in its belly; Its nurse*
> *is the Earth; It is origin of all. The*
> *consecration of the universe; Its*
> *inherent strength is perfected if it is*
> *turned into Earth.*

In this verse a single statement jumps out, whereby the wind carries the origin of all in its belly. We know winds on Earth are capable of moving many different things, both living and inert, but the next line helps narrow it down by saying the Earth nurses it. If transportation of Earth is ruled out from the wind's belly, that leaves the possibility of either water, micro-organisms, electricity, or a type of radiation. Even to say, the Earth nurses it, may infer Earth's ability to absorb water. To early alchemists, in continuing along an alchemical sense, the first two lines translate as: Its father is gold, its mother is silver.

Separate the Earth from Heaven; The
subtle from the gross
Gently and with great ingenuity it rises
from Earth to Heaven; And descends
again to Earth Thereby combining
within its; The power of both above and
the below.

Reading these lines from the tablet seems to point toward water being a key substance here. Earth and Heaven are indeed separate, and when looked at as a whole of the planet, water may also be a grossly overlooked subtlety vitally important to life as we know it. Water rises to the heavens in the form of evaporation and then falls back to Earth in the form of rain or snow. For either to occur, water molecules need to adhere to dust particles and micro organisms in the atmosphere, and it is at this point where water combines the power of both above and below. In an alchemical sense, one might interpret the Earth should now be physically separated from heaven, allowing the Earth to ascend and descend to obtain its properties.

Thus you will obtain the glory of the
whole universe; All obscurity will be clear
to you; This is the greatest force of all
powers because it overcomes every subtle
thing, And penetrates every solid thing;
In this way was the universe created;
From this will come many wondrous
applications, Because this is the pattern
Therefore am I called thrice Greatest
Hermes;Having all three parts of the
wisdom of the whole universe, Herein
have I completely explained the operation
of the sun.

Now it's to say, that by completing the tablet steps as an alchemy process we may find the ultimate knowledge, the answer to everything and how it's derived from one source, explaining how the universe was created. This is further bolstered by the suggestion of many wondrous applications, the discovery of a distinct pattern, and worded as an operation of gold. Yet, in a spiritual sense we find a similar outcome that in the deepest understanding of all things may we become clairvoyant and one with universal knowledge; Suggesting everything we know, and our souls, are entirely the byproduct of conscious mind and its source of light.

J.C. Vintner

Mysteries of the Universe

Throughout the course of life we are given signs designed to help us along the way, and even if those signs seem to steer us away from immediate desires, many believe they keep us on the correct course – *When listened to*. However we attempt to determine the true purpose of life, why we're here, or where we came from, we discover in our own hearts that we're on Earth by no accident all. It's a reason beyond explanation by any scientific formula with no words capable of encompassing the vastness of beauty it portrays. Life might not have started this way billions of years ago, but it has brought us to this moment unconditionally.

Energy endures through thick and thin.

Even-though we are partway through our own lives, our souls may feel as weathered as the moments after a long journey. They're very much alive; Wide awake in harmony with the ultimate serenity of our universe. Science and spirituality share similar concepts in the quest for truth. Undoubtedly we must explore every last possibility, be it science or spiritual in nature, before claiming anything is impossible. We are human and we are the only animals on planet Earth with a completely unparalleled form of intelligence.

It' nay be difficult to understand why life happens the way it does beyond any scientific or spiritual measure, or how we're able to cope with overwhelming emotions that seem destined to rip us apart. The valiant perplexity of life can bring us to from the darkest corners on the brim of apocalypse to pleasant feelings of peace and reassurance without hesitation. Everything we can remember over a lifetime is filled with mixed emotions although most favor positive memories as they help define our happiness. At a certain point these jumbled recollections of the past form together to create the person we know today, and it is calmness therein which strengthens our souls knowing one day life must come full circle for us as well.

Together moments throughout our lives build a foundation which helps to awaken our conscious selves, opening doorways of desire to learn, live, and ultimately be *happy*. It's a privilege to be given life, experience its awesome beauty, and to understand just how much that matters in the overall picture.

There will always be uneasy emotions filled with discontent waiting for opportune moments to strike anywhere throughout the cosmos, they follow the conscious awakening on the sidelines. Like a bittersweet reoccurring reminder designed to put emphasis on the necessity of balance in life, consciousness thrives within the soul.

Omnipresence of soul can be a reminder of general lessons in physics, how energy cannot be created or destroyed, that it just moves on and never disappears while always shifting forms to continue along its predestined path. Existence also seems similar to this physics concept in the sense that as life is introduced, life is also taken away, but it continues to flourish against all odds in the realm we are consciously aware of. It would be very strange if we could be prove the soul travels through alternate dimensions by science in order to facilitate its journey as that which life might be capable of.

Life replaces life and the soul lives on, they are harmonious together. The energy cannot destroyed so it must carry on by any means possible. This concept hints at a practical scientific reason for why some of us believe we've lived life on Earth before as another person, or why we sometimes feel an instantaneous connection with someone we've never met. Perhaps a trick to life is discovering how to reveal memories of our soul which goes beyond the thoughts of our mind.

As energy moves on, so do our lives, and always for different purposes according to principal understanding. Life as we know it, subconsciously, thrives interconnected through a complex network of quantum entanglement only truly appreciated by the spirituality of our emotion. By the breath of our soul, life brings about a variety of tribulations designed to help our spirits grow over the years, it has tests us by hardship and rewards us with blissful knowledge; life is faithful to nature's balance.

Our souls are life,
Our souls are who we are.

The Great Expanse

Science defines the universe as the result of tiny dense point exploding in the night sky around 13.7 billion years ago. The singularity before its presumed violent paroxysm measured roughly the size of an atom. A highly compacted object sets off a chain reaction, lasting only fractions of a milliseconds, ejecting all known existence from a single immense blast. For sake of simplicity, science appropriately named the event as the big-bang.

Our cosmos in their entirety were born as this fallout stretched far beyond the detonation point in all directions like an infinitely large ever-expanding balloon. With nearly limitless capacity, the balloon rapidly inflates over an immeasurable distance. Wake from this super cosmic wave facilitated creation of galaxies, planets, particles, star dust, and countless unexplained byproducts.

Everything we're aware of was called into existence with a force so strong that even gravity formed to create a basic framework for life to build upon. Include many bazaar exotic forms of reality which we have yet to discover, along with realities we only have an inkling of existing, and the universe becomes so unbelievably large that language even struggles to describe it.

Imagine if the known universe maintains equilibrium on an arm of a larger spiral universe as our solar system does in the Milky Way galaxy. At the point where light-years seem like micrometers it's extremely difficult for anyone to attempt assigning numbers capable of measuring the potential vastness of space.

Universes upon universes, upon universes.

All matter, created from the big bang and since, is believed to participate in a continuous physical cycle of death and birth. Energy is transformed from one existence into another indefinitely. Much like the birth of the universe and creation of the elements, the cycle of energy repeats for such a long time until one day it transforms into the foundation of life on planet Earth. Science explains evolution of life by tracing our ancestry back to single cell organisms just as it can pinpoint all of known existence back to a single cataclysmic cosmic event. We can refer to this moment as the Big Bang of Life on Earth.

In a brief moment many millions of years ago a single cell divided, triggering a long development phase growing complex systems in the process. A single cell transformed into a living, breathing, conscientious system composed of many millions of cells which suggestively mimics stars throughout our cosmos. They too formed with a primary directive of survival, reproduction, and environmental dominance.

The creation of the universe and all of life is not by accident, there must be purpose to it, even if comprehending that purpose is currently beyond human capability. Do complex systems realize they are continuously recycling energy on behalf of the universe simply by transforming it from one existence to another? This energetic connection lasts only for a brief few moments during the universal time-line before our physical body expires, dispersing any borrowed energy back into the universal collective through various forms.

Humans are conscious beings composed of millions of cells.

Do any of those individual cells possess full or partial awareness that perhaps mankind is unaware of, or is unable to detect with modern technology? We know cells communicate with each other using signaling to perform tasks on a regular basis similar to how ants behave, and we understand the mechanism, but we're unable to partake in an intelligent conversation with those signals at the cellular level. Nature creates complex living beings from millions upon millions of cells clearly resulting in a biological form capable of conscientious behavior while opening a realm of deeply spiritual subconscious awareness.

Through this perception it's entirely plausible cells have a conscious awareness, or at least in the very minimum, part of the necessary components for creating consciousness. Nature programs life on all levels with the ability to make choices based on environmental stimuli and that alone is amazing insight into how the universe works.

Time before physical transition is filled with the continuous cycle of spending and obtaining energy through various methods; Essentially life exerts energy in order to satisfy intake requirements while abiding by core directives. Energy transfer likely is the most critical hard-coded mechanism necessary for survival considering that energy is the vital ingredient for life's existence.

All life is animated by energy and as far as we know it's been this way since the birth of the universe. If all living organisms are variant energy constructs, then striving to obtain more energy must have an important significance on a level beyond that of any conscious realm. Replication is key here as it ensures the animation continues along with energy transformations, long after life expectancy of biological matter. It begins when two partially complete cells are thrust into a void with little guidance to reach each other, and when these cells eventually meet in conception, one is absorbed to transmit genetic code building blocks. Together they multiply through division and grow larger.

Eventually division replicates so many cells that another energy transformation creature is created. From the moment of the big bang in the beginning of existence, life demonstrates a contingency on growth by divisions of physical matter for survival. Maybe it's possible that reproductive systems of life on Earth parallel creation of all things known in the living universe. Basic elements of nature and its creation are not superfluous, they constantly maintain a significance of efficiency throughout all known realms to our knowledge; Even when one system may be less efficient compared to another.

The universe will find balance.

Consider genetic code, full of on-off switches as the principal set of instructions defining characteristic paths for cells to follow. The code is created at some point, but when and why? We know a variety of elements influence how DNA is written such as environmental conditions over long periods of time and hereditary traits, but we do not know what's responsible for creating the new slate with beginning markers. Does all life throughout the universe have DNA or is it only specific to life found on Earth? Is it a gift from a great architect or did extraterrestrials visit the Earth billions of years ago to create a lab experiment? Nobody has discovered the origin of DNA yet and implications of such a find may provide us with an answer to the ultimate question; Why we are here.

Think for one moment.

A single strand of uncoiled DNA measures approximately six feet in length and is compacted into a cell nucleus on the average size 6 micrometers. This equates to approximately 1,828,800 micrometers of DNA tightly packed inside the nucleus of a cell for an incredible 304,800 to one compression ratio. *Talk about efficiency!* Imagine the gigantic size of material from all of the universe compacted into a tiny, barely visible, dot in the distant sky.

Is there a similarity between the origins of the universe and cells found in living beings? It's quite possible now to imagine a very large amount of material compressed inside this dense point exploding outward to fill the universe. The super dense composition tightly packed matter containing all necessary elements for planetary structures, living beings, and the space between.

Maybe the building blocks of the universe also coiled around like DNA in a type of double helix configuration to efficiently occupy the structure from which existence was born. What even held the structure together, and does science know what triggered the event by observing the oldest known light in the universe?

Suppose the elements of the universe act in a similar way to cells in a human body by fusing together to create a single conscious being. In this case, the universe most likely exhibits its own version of consciousness, as a whole, by the collective of matter that defines it. We are conscious beings and a partial fraction of the whole of the universe, in terms of physical size, yet we are a large part of what defines it to ourselves.

Until we discover life elsewhere in space, we are the only ones defining what the universe is.

We define our existence. We classify and organize everything as one of our hard coded mechanisms for survival on Earth. It enables us to understand our environment through communicable language in symmetry with conscious awareness. As far as consciousness is able to look inward, it must also be able to look outward in an equal relation. Meaning that since we are able to look to the smallest of objects such as an atom, then we must also be able to look at to objects beyond our current perception of reality. Yes, even those objects presumably larger than the known universe.

The concept is very similar to a Matryoshka nesting doll. When the doll is opened up, a similar and smaller doll is found inside which reveals a similar and smaller doll, and so on. Could existence of life on Earth really be nestled into one of many layers inside a Matryoshka universe along with our thought perception of reality? Quantum mechanics offers a theoretical solution involving parallel worlds and time-lines; perhaps the universe might exist as an infinite number of layers itself, which are infinitely layered inside other universes.

Tiny particles composing all of existence can be found in infinitely strange configurations, which test theoretical science to the brink of disbelief – *All the while proving our universe is capable of anything our minds can imagine*. It's very perplexing to determine how we could access these realms by scientific explanation or not, but maybe there is a possible answer.

Discovering a way of expanding human consciousness to create a direct link to a universal consciousness is one method conceived by our ancient ancestors; Some even went to great lengths in attempt to achieve it. According to history books, the idea of Universal Mind was first purposed around 430 BCE by an ancient Greek philosopher named Anaxagoras. His cosmological theory states that all things existed from the start but in very small versions sizes of themselves. Over time the parts were brought together to create complex masses by the "motion of Mind."

Anaxagoras' philosophy encompasses multiple dimensional perception with a means of describing the universe, its composition, and how everything that exists relates to each other. Cosmological theory is intriguing when applied to the structure of life, that we are a collection of cells, or smaller versions of ourselves, just as a desert is a collection of sand particles. This philosophy also hints at the complexity of human thought and how we perceive the universe while living on a planet made of billions of tons of smaller versions of itself.

Great water bodies composing 70% of the Earth's surface are made with an incredible amount of individual water droplets meshed together the same as billions upon billions of mist particles forming in the skies above to create beautiful, fluffy clouds.

Anaxagoras tells us we are products of ourselves and that the Universal Mind brings all of the smaller parts together to create the complex existence we describe as reality. Maybe it's possible to access the Universal Mind and tap into its collection of knowledge, as vast as the universe is large.

Perhaps we create our own existence by combining smaller versions of everything as a means to manifest our known reality.

Metaphysical Life

Studies of ancient civilizations tend to point toward a common inclusion of psychoactive substances for ritualistic purposes in everyday life. Chemicals were often used to aid subjects in meditation for spiritual awakening while acting as a bridge from human consciousness to the deities. Shamanism traditionally finds its home in South America where the Moche, Nazca, Inca, Maya, Olmec and Aztec cultures participated in rituals involving San Pedro cactus to induce visions; However, Shaman are not exclusive to the area. Variations of medicine man healers are found throughout the world from Asia to Africa and North America.

The idea of a spiritual healer, or medicine man, is a common belief for most ancient cultures and many of their traditions are still practiced to this day. A shaman is capable of communicating with the spirit world in order to diagnose major illnesses and other ailments while maintaining the belief of an interconnected living universe accessible by mythic journeys into the subconscious. Cacti are just one of many substances used to reach states of higher consciousness.

Several ancient cultures including the Egyptians, Greeks, Mycenaean, Vedics, and Urarina, utilized combinations of psychoactive substances in order to achieve an enhanced state of being. The basic concept is that mind altering drugs disassociate the consciousness from the physical realm and allow it to absorb or even interact with the realm beyond. Psychoactive substances can trigger euphoria and theoretical connections to subconscious realms because of their effect on neurons in the brain. If chemical ingestion results in repetitive behavior of neurons, it may explain how they alter the mind's perception of reality.

Communicating the mind's subconscious while awake is something long desired by many civilizations for thousands of years. Discovering an effective means of relaying information proves to be a difficult task. Dreaming may offer a glimpse into the possibility of communicating with the subconscious. Deciphering how thoughts manifest in the brain during sleep also proves difficult, but there are clues to how it happens. For instance, while in a preliminary dreaming state prior to REM stage, breathing and neural activities follow a rhythmic pattern with subtle spikes in activity once in a while. The rhythm breaks and becomes very irregular when REM phase is reached. Sleep stages before and after rapid eye movement may indicate exactly how and why it happens.

Is REM state the subconscious mind's ability of reaching enlightenment during rest periods? Perhaps each time a person falls asleep their subconscious utilizes rhythmic processes to establish a connection to the mind as a form of conscious regeneration from a higher level. There is also an idea floating around that we are dreaming all the time even while we're awake, that our reality is actuality in a dreaming state – *and possibly why some dreams are so vivid they feel absolutely real.*

Normally ritualistic practices involve a type of rhythmic process to enter a trance-like state with the ultimate goal of enlightenment. Music, chanting and repetitive physical motions help facilitate a journey into the subconscious while putting the mind at ease. Repetition seems to unlock a door to the mind's eye by allowing the subject to peer into an otherworldly experience. Freud explains compulsion to repeat as a more primitive, elementary, and instinctual behavioral pattern which overrides even the organism's search for pleasure. Do conditioning responses of repetition teach an organism on a subconscious level a reward greater than pleasure itself, or are humans instinctively conditioned for achieving spiritual connection with the universe? Neurotheologians believe this might be the case.

By studying the brain, and how religious beliefs alter a patient's state of mind, neuroscience has possibly discovered a spiritual module in the human brain. The neural substrate in question is a biological center of emotion called the limbic system. If a connection between the limbic system or any other part of the brain is proven to be influenced by spiritual belief, then Neurotheology might be able to prove scientifically that humans have a spiritual predisposition hard-coded into the brain from the moment of birth. The outcome of these studies present as both inconsequential (to skeptics) and comforting for many of those who already believe in a spiritual connection with God and the universe from their moment of existence.

In what means does subconscious interact with a Universal Mind? Altered mind state, deep sleep dreaming, near death experiences, post-traumatic stress, and clairvoyant situations constantly hint at the presence of something beyond the realm of physical experience. Unexplainable coincidences at times are so bountiful that it seems like the universe is trying to communicate with us directly. To teach and share, or warn us of dangers. The resulting scenarios play repeatedly inside the mind often with an overwhelming urge to deduce their meaning through quantum process of potential outcomes.

Coincidences are an important part of life even if they don't seem to provide a direct measurable outcome. Would life exist without coincidence? Mathematical probability suggests coincidental events take place so frequently that the most astonishing of coincidences would be a time when they don't happen at all.

Even though statisticians assure the general public that coincidences do not have a spiritual significance, many still follow the path that coincidence creates.

Such events can become too important to ignore as they ultimately emphasize significance to a spiritual believer. It's also possible coincidental events are evidence of clairvoyant reaction in connectivity with the subconscious realms. Each event brings a new message, rehashes an old message, or builds upon familiarities between images stored inside the mind and what is presently occurring in our physical realm.

Whether an event triggers a past thought or creates a new one, there is a definite feeling of significance over matter. After the event (*and possibly thought spiraling*) the mind may become weak or tired from a heightened sense of awareness which requires anywhere from several minutes to several days to recover. A great deal of concentration and meditation is necessary for some to reach a sixth sense of clairvoyance while others may happen upon it more easily.

Perhaps coincidences, when pursued with pure honest intent, are initial seeds that allow the human mind to grow with its physical realm. People refer to these situations not only as clairvoyant encounters, but also as Karma, Vipaka, and Déjà Vu depending on how they manifest. Aside from clairvoyance, a coincidental event by *"cause and effect"* guides a person who tends to believe their direct actions with Karma are responsible for future results by Vipaka.

A coincidence might also affect the mind by believing a certain situation happened once before and is currently repeating for an unknown reason. Sometimes these moments stimulate the mind enough to trigger an epiphany related specifically to personal spiritual discovery. When consciousness is presented with a subconscious puzzle, and a solution to the puzzle is found, the mind becomes capable of taking addictive spiritual leaps. *In this sense life is, in essence, a casualty of consciousness.* On-line video gamers sometimes refer to these moments of Déjà Vu as the time when a character re-spawns after a virtual death; Perhaps suggesting the instant of epiphany is an agreement or syncing of the conscious and subconscious realms.

Realization sets the truth free.

Life on Earth appears dependent on connectivity to universe through quantum entanglement, where a chain reaction of cause and effect manages to alter the outcome of each organism's immediate future. The changes can be subtle and sometimes go unnoticed amongst the masses which is all part of the universe rearranging and reorganizing itself into the most efficient state of balance possible. Perhaps this happens as a method of herding energy to desired locations as deemed necessary by the master construct.

People have the power to help each other, and the universe, by entertaining the beautiful quantum properties of life. Paying it forward, distributing positive vibes, being attentive to Karma, and seeking to help each other are ways of tugging on the microscopic string that binds everything in the universe. The string connects every living organism and every assumed inanimate object to every corner of the universe.

Our ancestors practiced spiritual rituals on a daily basis paying homage to the gods with intent of solidifying their future. Dancing for rain to nurture crops, which in turn fed the population. Making pilgrimages to display a deep respect for family, gods, and the Earth. Some cultures even went so far as practicing ritual sacrifice to appease gods for survival.

Many spiritual traditions still exist in the modern world, demonstrating a continual enlightened awareness throughout the ages designed to change the potential outcomes of human future, because they believe spirituality is the key to reality. If everyone helped spread good fortune and performed positive deeds regularly, there would be no room in the world for negativity to fester.

Monopole Birth

Backing up a few steps to stimulate the conscious mind and discover *an idea in contemplation of the relationship between conscious realms and their origin*. Back to those points about inception of the universe and how its creation may not be quite as convenient as science explains. Imagine the insurmountable level of potential energy built up inside the singularity which created the known universe. When the dense ball of singularity matter exploded, if that's how it took place, the dense point must have possessed its own charge(s) right? Quadrupole?

Nearly everything mankind has ever documented is known to hold some type of charge as a property of energetic alignment in the universe. Positive, negative, neutral. Gravity is relative to mass and science knows the object responsible for detonating the big bang had an incredible amount of it. Along with gravitational fields are magnetic fields which are responsible for aligning the components of mass traditionally in a north/south configuration.

Suppose the original ball of matter was so massive and so dense that its magnetic properties actually resembled that of the fabled quantum monopole? During the explosion ejecta flew further and further away while maintaining energy in both momentum and its own physical makeup. Over time new objects evolved from basic properties of the singularity origin by taking on mass, gravitational pull, and multiple pole magnetic properties.

Moments before ignition, inside the singularity's core, building blocks for the entire universe coalesce in anticipation of their destiny. Presumably these blocks are are held together by strong molecular links, an enhanced version of gravity, or an altered form of magnetism. At the time of the blast, these links distort beyond physical capability as they're forced into each other at unfathomable pressures – *Snap!*

The molecular links pull apart and are suddenly no longer holding the object together by its internal structure. It triggers rapid expansion, eventually spewing contents across enormous distances in the vacuum of space in every possible direction. The bonds themselves stretch into great voids presently described as the deep, cold, and dark space. Inner materials fleeing from the explosion continue gaining acceleration, as they too expand, and their only competition for occupation of space are the links which once held them tight. Eventually the expansion causes free connective materials to inadvertently contact their counterparts once again.

This event has multiple adverse effects. Connective molecules continue expanding away from their origin while pushing inner materials outward in sync with the initial momentum force relative to the bond snapping in the beginning. Molecular links continue to follow their hard-coded construct. They attempt to reattach to the inner materials, creating a steady resistance that begins to slow the acceleration rate of expansion. Collaborative energy levels drop substantially over time since everything ejected from ground zero traveled enormous distances. The further matter travels by this scenario, the further its symbiotic connection with energy is stretched. Fuel is lost as energy transfers to forms of heat and radiation – *Energy dwindles like a flickering candle in a delicate breeze.*

Eventually newborn matter is confronted with an energy problem as resources deplete to a level so low that matter must turn to alternate survival mechanisms. If more energy is not introduced into the system to compensate for expansion, decay processes take over, materials along with their linking matter become inactive over time and the energy moves on. Since energy cannot be created, new processes are required to combat the decay. Such processes are similar to those designed to harvest energy and store it for later consumption. Something humans have learned to be an invaluable long-term survival tactic.

Connective bonds in the void of space might resemble the controversial substance known as Dark Energy incidentally acting as an accurate counterpart to Light Energy. Inner materials adapt to become a predominate resource by outnumbering their links only by a factor of one. It's far more complex than a good versus evil or dark versus light scenario. The two exist as counterpart byproducts of the monopole, whereas one could not exist without the other. Theoretically, two points in space are held together by one link at minimum. When all points are separated from each other, one less link than the number of overall points remains due to this property. Like a positive and negative magnet, they are attracted to each other with a force so strong that if combined once again, the monopole which originally gave birth would be recreated, thus completing the cycle.

Currently the monopole is a hypothetical particle purposed in super-string theory. Implications of a particle with only one magnetic pole would forever change the world and completely alter the perspective of how life works.

Quantum physics highly suggests such a particle does exist just as the Higgs Boson. Given the idea of the universe being created from a single dense point billions of years ago, and purposed as that singularity being a monopole particle, perhaps the universe has been trying to pull itself back together since the big bang.

After splitting into millions upon trillions of particles and expanding outward at unfathomable speeds, will the universe one day begin to contract and pull everything back to the source? Was ejecta embedded with North-South attracting poles for this reason and is it possible that gravitational fields are using mass to collect light and dark matter as a herding mechanism preemptive to a great collapse? If so, then the presence of gravity indicates the process has passed development phase, but it will not accelerate until contraction pulls matter closer together for gravity to collect.

The next big question is if there really was only a single point from which the universe came to light. Is it possible the big bang resulted from the fusing of two points, or two monopoles, which became one and then rapidly divided in an explosion to form the known universe? When examining all known living creatures and plants on Earth, it is very evident life seems to rely on a pairing organization. Cells divide into pairs and pairs upon pairs to create living, breathing organisms which populate the planet. Magnetism works fundamentally on an opposite north and south pairing field orientation. Electricity flows in an opposite pairing from positives to negatives.

Physical light and darkness pair to create a variance in perceptive realms. Temperature and the exchange of heat balances on a pairing scale from freezing to burning. Man's understanding of reality by logic operates on principle pairing, on or off. There are numerous examples of how pairing is important to the function of life and the universe, but in the next part of this theory, emphasis primarily focuses on animal reproduction. Replicating animals usually require mating pairs to deliver cells destined to fuse together and begin a division pairing process to create living, breathing, reproducing entities. In order for animals to multiply, cells must divide.

Survival of the majority of organisms on Earth requires, for the most part, a pair of opposite genders interacting to transfer cells for replication. The cells each carry part of the necessary building block information for life passed down from generation to generation. When the mated cells combine, a new life form is born through its division. The organism then spends a lifetime gathering and recycling energy to replicate and eventually transition at death. Young life demonstrates an over-abundance of energy at an early age which seems to provide necessary momentum for learning and growth toward reproduction.

Evidently enough the cycle of life is also a pairing system from birth to death on borrowed energy. Why would the universe choose to extend itself in this manor, if at all given a choice in the matter? To create energy constructs dependent on their species for means of survival?

Lets say, in the far chance of a cataclysmic event leaving only a few living beings behind, if for any reason those beings could not reproduce then the entire species would become extinct. Unless of course in the case of such animals like frogs capable of changing sex under nearly impossible survival conditions. Given the most extreme scenario, a lack in living organisms may require the universe to exchange methods for transporting and recycling energy into another form just as frogs adapt.

Pairing behavior of cells is eerily similar to the attraction properties of north and south magnetic poles and the flow of electricity in modern devices. For most cases the birth of a living being is a result of a union between two counterpart cells. Just as the known magnetic field structure requires an attraction of poles to be complete, the birth of a living organism often requires the attraction of two cells. A major difference, though, is that two biological cells eventually meet to create life whereas magnetic poles are constantly in a never ending cycle trying to catch each other. The association between living cells and magnetic fields is the subtle display of attraction in unison with the universe attempting to pull itself back together. Is it possible that asexual organisms mimic the theorized monopole given this comparative scenario.

Asexual organisms are simply the masters of reproductive efficiency.

Life on Earth continues energy recycling methods millions and millions of years in the making. Genes pass down from generation to generation as life adapts to a constantly changing environment. Reproduction for many organisms follows along a similar path as the birth of the universe. When two counterpart cells meet, they absorb and divide to create a living entity in an explosion of cells. Does this possibly hint at the fact the birth of the universe may have started in a similar fashion?

Was the purposed single dense point in the sky actually a collection of smaller points rapidly dividing until its constraints could no longer hold, causing an eruption of cells to fly throughout the cosmos after a violent explosion? Examining this idea is imperative to understand how science currently envisions life in the modern world. Inventions like the microscope and telescope opened vast previously unseen worlds, and placed their access into the palm of human hands. Science is accustomed to looking inward at the material makeup of elements to propose function, predict results, and control environments.

Only recently in the grand scheme of things has science attempted to examine just how large this scale might be. The universe is defined as a collection of everything from living beings inhabiting the Earth's surface to the many billions of stars observed in the night sky. Understanding materials that compose the universe may help mankind to discover answers to the ultimate questions of existence, and change the course of human history forever.

Order in Chaos

Chaturanga, the earliest assumed known form of Chess was invented in the 6th century CE, in India after a battle formation found in the Mahabharata, well before it's modern counterpart found life in Europe. The game is played on a board named Ashtapada, dating well before the 6th century as a dice game, which is cited by the Vinayapitaka and Suyagadamga texts as a game Buddha must keep his distance from.

It's believed these dice games, as well as Chaturanga, could inspire violent behavior in turn leading Buddha away from the path to enlightenment. Rightfully so, considering the game strategy in Chess relies on defeating your opponents in a controlled battle as originally intended.

No doubt the losing side wouldn't be too pleased if they lost their army and the same goes for anyone gambling on the earlier dice versions. The point however is nestled behind war strategies in making a series of moves contingent on each other, a practical example of cause and effect. Game theory is a way of taking a seemingly chaotic mess and turning it into an advantage by defeating the enemy in small consequential steps at a time.

It's an appropriate method in the context of war, especially when it allows an opponent with less resources to overcome the odds with a great game plan.

Although we're unsure exactly when the Ashtapada was invented, there are cuneiform references of a similar nature in ancient history dating as far back as 3,000 years BCE during the time of the Sumerian culture. The Epic of Creation mentions Anunnaki as responsible for changing the outcome of human future indirectly in result of their activities, suggesting the gods actions produce unintentional byproducts which alter the fate of mankind.

In a similar fashion, if the concept is deliberate, it alludes the Anunnaki are participating in a game of Chess amongst themselves where each piece moved intentionally affects people on Earth, perhaps even through a type of quantum entanglement.

Their efforts are directed in different locations throughout the universe and the actions are affecting mankind in adverse ways. It's the Sumerian understanding for random events found throughout life and it helps bring order to chaos found all around us, or at least it offers possible justification why random events happen. According to the Anunnaki in this case, life is not really random or chaotic, the deliberate events are really preconceived notions of gods at war calculating every, last, possible quantum outcome to achieve success.

Deciphering chaos requires an intuitive understanding of theoretical physics and those three laws put into place nearly two centuries ago by Sir Isaac Newton, the Laws of motion. Mathematics is capable of providing solutions to complex problems provided there is sufficient data to apply values to constants and variables involved in the equations, but can physics answers describe events responsible for system-wide changes?

For example, pool balls neatly set in a triangle formation on a felt table are broken by a cue ball, relaying force from the pool cue, which causes the numbered spheres to scatter around the table, each relaying part of the initial force with respect to the laws of physics, until eventually each ball comes to rest. Now imagine trying to put those balls back into formation using only their mathematical trajectories and by solving for the momentum forces responsible. Then take away any knowledge of a pool cue being the principal catalyst. How can the system be solved and would science be able to determine what caused the pool balls to break their formation, at what force, and why?

Perception is critical in deciphering the origins of the universe because we understand through astronomy the basic state of the universe today and where it was millions of years ago by determining positions of stars and galaxies.

However, we don't know anything of a universe pool cue responsible for triggering the singularity which then scattered particles into place – *Simply put, what made the big bang go bang?* In the pool table scenario we are only looking at the cue-ball as the Big Bang due to the fact that the ball carried forth the initial force which drove apart the elements responsible for creating the universe today. Take away assumed knowledge of the pool cue and theories turn into speculations of what actually moved the cue-ball into place.

Physics only provides enough information to accurately reconstruct scenarios provided there is sufficient data to apply to each and every chaotic or non chaotic result. Meaning, unless mankind is able to discover the pool cue itself, determine its function, and prove its relation to the Big Bang, we may not be able to understand where the universe came from or why we're here. Unfortunately this is a very chilling reality in the field of applied sciences because it's like trying to solve a homicide contingent on placing a murder weapon, except that murder weapon does not exist physically in our current reality. Going a step further after taking away the pool cue, we take away the organized neatly stacked and numbered triangle, another assumed reality. We are left with a group of pool balls that may or may not have interacted with each other at some point and may or may not have physical relationships with each other, be it through string theory or other means.

Science can create relationships, measure distances, measure forces, and even suggest possible organized solutions based on the current state of pool balls in attempt to satisfy curiosities. Religion can suggest answers to the problem by claiming there must be a purpose, or that it's the way nature intended for it to be, or that we're not meant to understand.

Both disciplines are unable to provide a definitive solution since too much information is absent from the equation. Suppose humanity followed tracks of an unknown animal for thousands of years, all they know of that animal are by the tracks and the rest is left up to speculation. Those tracks would be compared to other animals in the identification process, suggesting possible explanations, and perhaps once in a while individuals might begin to believe they caught a glimpse of the animal to help justify speculations. Until the animal is found, science can only guess what it might be.

A branch of mathematics, called Chaos Theory, is working to compensate for the unknown variables in the universe by determining a statistical curve of data that best fits the current models. When applied to certain scenarios, Chaos theory becomes a very powerful tool for predicting possible outcomes, and if unlocked completely it would change the world forever. Plugging in systems data for wave-lines breaking on beaches or leaves falling from trees provides enough information to Chaos Theory to predict where the wave will break, or where the leaf will land on the ground. It's a bit like determining asteroid impacts to planets by only knowing the positions of the asteroid and planet then adding in environmental data to calculate the outcome.

Computer modeling programs are capable of solving lesser situations which seem potentially chaotic with known dynamic theories such as asteroid impacts, however, science is still working on organizing highly chaotic systems with several unknown dynamics.

For example, solving chaotic theory would allow a person to draw a curve that best fits the stock market and lottery drawings, thus accurately predicting the stock price or winning numbers on any given day to 100% accuracy. Devastating to the world economies depending on stock and lottery money, yet beneficial for predicting disasters, saving lives, and planning for the future of humanity throughout the universe.

As appealing as discovering a solution Chaos is, it also means determining every specific piece of information along the line, how it interacts with each other in every conceivable notion, and what its impact is on the overall system. The answer may provide mankind with the ability to move forward through multiple dimensions instantaneously, compensating for potentially dangerous implications by propelling man into the future.

The Scope of Nature

Looking far into the distance proved to be a valuable asset to 17th century armies for gathering real-time intelligence without tipping off the enemy. Ship captains found themselves in distinct advantage with the help of a looking glass to find land, spot bad weather, or discover other vessels lurking in the vicinity. In the midst of the turmoils of war, Galileo turned a primitive telescope toward Earth's moon to discover a rocky surface covered in craters. The moment must have felt astonishing considering accepted beliefs in the 17th century stated the moon was smooth as seen by the naked eye on Earth. Galileo documented his observations in great detail and revolutionized scientific understanding of the cosmos.

Years later, Issac Newton refined the telescope to include a reflecting mirror with an eye-piece allowing a more comfortable method of viewing while removing chromatic aberration color distortions from the image. Over time the size of image magnifications increased exponentially with larger telescopes, creating a whole new untapped method of discovery. Some scientists began frantically searching the night sky while a few turned magnification into a revolutionary way of looking inward.

Microscopes peer into incredible worlds barely visible (or not at all visible) to unaided human vision. They're capable of examining structures of cells, proteins, particles, DNA, and atoms in fine detail. Microscopes enable construction tiny machines with nanotechnology. They help reconstruct, dissect, or create chemical elements. Advances in disease control, medications, and antidotes all rely on the performance of microscopes.

Life is teeming with building blocks upon building blocks inside of building blocks which constantly seems to spiral infinitely inward as human technology improves. Just as Matryoshka nesting elements. If this is the case, as the further one looks inside they will continue to find more information, then it must also be true for the opposite. Looking outward with a telescope, science attempts to understand the sheer monstrosity of existence. Worlds are different from this point of view and their components come across to be further wide-spread than previously imagined. There is a relation; A harmony existing between the size of the visible universe and the size of the universe which cannot be seen.

Consider if humankind moved along scale and size of living organisms to comparatively, an ant colony. The psychology of ants and their social structure is different, but there is a similarity to how ants may perceive the world. If they stopped to philosophize over the meaning of life, why they exist, and where they came from, would they be able to find an answer? An ant looking inward with a microscope performing surgeries on other ants could be considered microsurgery when compared to human counterparts.

The same ant looking outward with a telescope would see worlds that humans commonly describe as street lights, air planes, and construction cranes for example. Now if the same ants tried to decipher their meaning of existence by studying their makeup and the environment around them, they would probably come to a different conclusion compared to humans given the same situation.

With a little imagination humans are able to look at themselves in the position of an ant colony and see a scope of life from the smallest to the largest. What it begins to explain is that even-though saying the universe is unimaginably large, it is actually much larger than consciously fathomable. Modern telescopes can examine narrow bands of light in the sky which in reality are billions of times bigger than the images initially describe.

Perhaps the clue here is discovering a means to exploring outward beyond conventional telescopes to build an image of what the universe may be in its entirety as a collective of all life, planets, and everything between. If ants tried to capture an image of the world they live in, how would they do it? A shuttle to the top of a street light? What beyond there? Every question has an answer, but every answer leads to another question.

One way to discover what lies beyond the universe is to begin foundation work with our current technologies on distant planets beyond that of current deep space probes. The rough communication signal between the Spirit and Opportunity rovers landing on Mars averaged between 10 to 16 minutes to send operations data. Imagine how far away a NASA rover device could be if technology allowed years to communicate from Earth and back.

Consider how far Earth communications could reach if technology created repeater stations designed to launch into deep space and land on distant planets as well as hover in neutral gravity zones. Each device on the ground is equipped with a variety of surveying equipment powered by solar panels or small nuclear reactors. A satellite orbiting around the planet acts as unobstructed data repeaters linking the ground device to the space network. The satellite may also focus sunlight to the planet's surface by a mirror, extending available energy for the ground device. Primary directive is to contribute a communications signal boost from planet to planet much like the microwave towers and satellite transmitters around Earth.

Stable communications networks are critical to the advancement of human technology. Extending information exchange systems to span planets and their moons is laying the foundation for future endeavors on foreign worlds. Fixed-observation satellite telescopes with down-links to repeater stations strategically placed on distant planets add to the communications arsenal. Each telescope focuses on a specific part of the sky from the vantage point of said planet then relays information through the network backbone for computer analysis. Once several stations are in place, the telescopes may be used together in an array to look farther and deeper into the universe as never before possible. Kamikaze observation probes launched into deep space with no return? Orbit those probes around distant planets to relay data and form a network with each other.

The compliment of a deep space communication network is utilizing collaborative efforts of all scientific, religious, and theoretical disciplines on Earth to create a "mother-ship" of humanity. Undoubtedly this construction would be so massive, dwarfing all others known in the history of man. Science fiction along with UFO theories touch upon the mother-ship concept, but what if humanity turned that concept into an accomplished physical reality before it one day catches them by surprise?

During deployment of communication repeater terminals, construction of the massive vessel takes place. Resource materials are saved if built on the Earth's surface provided the logistics for launching are ironed out during the process. Building in space is another feasible option though it would save economically if the materials from rocket launches are somehow recycled in to ship components. World-wide collaboration may eliminate the need for a conventional money-driven economy by shifting common focus from personal gain to survival of the species. The point is, however, with the current technological expertise, population, intelligence levels and determination, such a project does not seem far fetched.

At the moment there isn't a master plan, at least a master plan known and practiced worldwide by the general public. People in the working world are concerned first-most with feeding families and keeping households running in a positive direction. Too many large corporations are fixated on padding company books with no innovative goals aside from growing business and making more money. The cycle from consumer to company to consumer fills time day to day but is not preparing the world for realistic future endeavors in space. Due to the expense and associated dangers, a very limited amount of civilian programs are available.

Money will not save the planet from a sudden catastrophe or an uncontrollable world-wide epidemic deeming the surface unlivable. Present day survivalists agree that resources such as gas, ammunition and food will become the desired currency in a time of global disaster if anyone survives the initial fallout.

On the contrary there is at least one very positive result of a global financial market pertaining to a human future in space. Companies and consumers have forced industry developments to excel by creating demands for revolutionary technologies. There are well known private sector companies spanning several countries running experiments in space, surveying, and even building a space station together. Men have stepped on the moon and satellites are monitoring the moons of distant planets. Stephen Hawking mentioned how mankind must take the leap into space in order to survive for the future within the next hundred years. Factors such as population growth, strains on resources, global climate changes, and unforeseen cataclysmic events further emphasize Hawking's message. There is a growing urgency to refine and perfect survival in space amongst new age thinkers and the world population needs to know how to deal with theoretical catastrophe before it's too late.

Technology and data is doubling at faster and faster rates each day, creeping towards a theoretical climax which some believe is a point where artificial intelligence manifests into an entity capable of learning and reproducing for itself without intervention. Several technologies have moved beyond their everyday practical realms for the average person.

Finding methods to apply technologies on larger and more sophisticated scales may prove to be successful for space survival over the long term. It's well understood that in order to take giant leaps, baby steps need to be placed first. Eventually society needs to get past those baby steps to be part of a much larger picture. Man walked on the moon out of curiosity, for the question if it could be done or not, and in the spirit of competition between nations. A place to explore without the burden of war. To our knowledge, this event did not happen as a preconceived planned step from a global collective master plan to explore and populate the universe.

The lunar lander does not currently serve as a functional communication device, nor has it sent data back to Earth over several years surveying the moon's processes, climate, or other vital information. It rests on the moon's surface bearing an inscription along with an American flag as proof that man successfully made the journey. This opened a door showing the world that it's indeed possible for humans to travel into space, and return to Earth, for the benefit of their own survival, but the equipment could be continuing the legacy by providing important data over the years as opposed to collecting moon dust on the surface.

Four Elements

A well known Aztec mythology, The Five Suns, follows along the same concept of four cardinal elements and four cardinal directions, though the directions in this case refer to the outcome of world eras. The first era under the Jaguar Sun, Nahui Ocelotl, animals on the planet were giants and devoured by jaguars. Interestingly, well known historical record tells us giant animals did once roam the planet as dinosaurs. Did Jaguars kill them? As in the Jaguar sense as Quetzalcoatl, who then became worshiped and revered by man for being saved?

During the era of the Wind Sun, Nahui Ehecatl, people became monkeys as the world was destroyed by hurricanes and tropical storms; This may be referring to a drastic change at the end of an ice age as global temperatures warm to create unstable violent weather patterns. In the era of the Rain Sun, Nahui Quiahuitl, life on Earth was destroyed by raining fire and all those who survived were birds, or became birds in order to survive. Perhaps the Rain sun could be translated as Fiery Sun, by the sounds of a super volcano eruption, or asteroid impact fire and brimstone fallout reaching the ends of the Earth. During the Water Sun, Nahui Atl, life on Earth became fish as the world perished in a great flood; As with legends in Sumerian texts and the Bible. The fifth sun, or Earthquake Sun, Nahui Ollin, is the current era in a time believed to be destroyed by earthquakes; This remains to be witnessed.

In ancient Aztec codices, Ometeotl is believed by some scholars as the supreme creator of Aztecs through translation, as a god of duality both male and female commonly known as Tonacatecuhtli and Tonacacihuatl, born out of the nothingness of space to create the universe. From Ometeotl, the four cardinal directions were established, each with a god to keep watch over. In the North, Tezcatlipoca, god of judgment, night, and sorcery, represented by the color Black. To the east, Xipe Totec, god of gold, farming, and spring, represented by the color Red. To the south, Huitzilopochtli, the god of war, represented by the color Blue. To the west, Quetzalcoatl, the god of light, mercy, and wind, represented by the color White. In Nahuatl language, Tletl the Fire, Ehekatl the Wind or Air, Atl the Water, and Tlalli the Earth represent Tiahuizlampa to the East, Mictlampa to the North, Huitzlampa to the South, and Cihuatlampa to the West respectively.

Tletl, element of Fire

Tletl is an element of power, the seeds of creation, and the direction of light and illumination. In nature, life grows from the aftermath of fire's destruction, fire creates and shapes existence. Fusion inside the sun converts Hydrogen to Helium nuclei which provides heat and light in the form of radiation bombarding Earth's atmosphere continuously. Mankind's evolution is by in part a result of the giant fiery sphere warming our planet. Egyptians undoubtedly recognized the importance of fire. A bringer of life as Seth, or Set. This is also evident in the channeling of RA, proclaiming the beginning of a grand cycle of life as fire and wind affect Earth and water in the First Density, to bring forth a Second Density as creation of all animals and plants. Fire is the Navel Chakra, Manipura in Buddhism and in Hinduism, Agni. In astrology, Fire is associated with Mars, and in the Zodiac with Aries, Leo, and Sagittarius.

Ehekatl, element of Air

Ehekatl is an element of freedom in the direction of elders, ancestors, and the spirit world. Wind resides as a place of rest, transformation, wisdom, reflection and communication. It is the great element of Mobility, capable of destruction, but also a bringer of life. Wind helps distribute seeds and pollen, allowing plants to reproduce, while providing necessary gas for animals, plants, and humans to breathe. Earth's atmosphere is a blanket of air protecting life from harsh radiation emitted from the cosmos. Ancient ancestors, elders, and occupants of the spirit world are able to travel through air and take on the form of wind; This might be a plausible explanation of why ghosts and spirits are believed to have air-like qualities and abilities. Air or Wind is known as Heru or Horus in Egyptian, the Heart Chakra, Anahata in Buddhism and in Hinduism, Marut. In the Zodiac, Air is associated with Gemini, Libra, and Aquarius.

Atl, element of Water

Atl is an element of change in the direction of youth, renewal, cleansing, and perseverance. Water is the great element of Fluidity and a vital resource for the existence of life. In many cultures, water is part of a sacred process of purification by which the body is cleansed. It is a source of nourishment for all living beings, capable of revitalizing the spirit, wakening consciousness, and reflecting the soul by meditative scrying in divination. Many scholars agree it is mankind's ability to control water flow through aqueduct, cistern, irrigation, and sewage systems that set the foundation for great technological advances in human history. Water is known as Ausar or Osiris in Egyptian, the Sacral Chakra, Svadhisthana in Buddhism, and in Hinduism, Jala. In the Zodiac, Water is associated with Cancer, Scorpio and Pisces.

Tlalli, element of Earth

Tlalli is an element of substance in the direction of intuitiveness, materialization, and mystery. It is the great element of Solidity, representing fertility of female energy, nurturing all of life, known as Mother Earth. Life is a combination of the four cardinal elements. Humans live upon it, transforming rock into materials for survival and a further understanding of their existence. Plants and animals find nourishment from minerals in soil; mankind utilizes the ground to cultivate food; It is a stable foundation from which life is built. The planet is perplexing under certain light, only then compounded by mankind's ability to construct marvelously mysterious monuments out of it. Physical creation is born of Earth and returned to it; Though, spiritual energy may pass through or with other elements in the cosmos. Earth is known as Auset or Isis in Egyptian, the Root Chakra, Muladhara in Buddhism, and in Hinduism, Kshiti. In the Zodiac, Earth is associated with Taurus, Virgo, and Capricorn.

Prints of the Past

Quantum theories suggest energy is made of very small units with elementary particles which behave like particles and waves at the same instant. The particle movement appears completely random while very difficult to calculate. Incidentally, quantum theory also purposes that the past, present, and future coherently exist at the exact same moment in time. In other words, current actions of humans are directly affecting both the past, present, and future at the same time.

There are *hundreds* of spin-off theories from this master concept ranging from humans indirectly changing their past unknowingly on a subconscious level, by time machine devices, or through deep spiritual connectivity. Given the purposed theories, quantum physics suggests an explanation for strange artifacts discovered throughout the world.

Current archaeological record indicates the oldest known foot prints of a human ancestor date around 3. 7 million years ago from a collection of eleven prints discovered in Laetoli, Tanzania. The oldest dinosaur footprints date roughly between 246-250 million years ago from an animal smaller than a house cat called the Spingopus. A discovery made in 1987 by Jerry McDonald tests theories stating that humans didn't live during the time of dinosaurs. He discovered a modern *human footprint* in Permian strata which dates to an estimated 290 million years ago. The fossil defies scientific logic and according to the Smithsonian the discovery was filed under problematic due to its bazaar implications. McDonald's footprint discovery is genuine and causes concern amongst the scientific community – *Where exactly is the link now?*

Even more puzzling are the fossils discovered in Fisher Canyon, Nevada, the Canadian Arctic, Africa, and in Delta, Utah. The imprint from Fisher Canyon resembles a modern size thirteen shoe including a line of double-sewed stitching fused into coal dating back 15 million years ago. Then in Africa, a gigantic 4 ft. long barefoot print is believed by some to be evidence of the giants discussed in the Bible; (There is a possibility the African giant print could be a very odd natural formation, though). In the Canadian Arctic, hand and finger prints were found in ancient limestone dating to nearly 110 million years ago. Finally, in a 300 to 600 million year old Utah shale deposit, archaeologists uncovered a human footprint which might be wearing a sandal. All four cases predate estimates of when the first humans walked the Earth by many millions of years, again troubling to modern science.

Many strange metal objects have been discovered throughout the world, also with their own puzzling circumstances. The Coso Artifact, found in 1961 just outside of Olancha, California, is a great example. Three gem hunters found what they thought was a geode and proceeded to break it open. Instead of finding a sparkling prismatic geode inside, there was a milky white object resembling porcelain construction. An x-ray on the object revealed a metal shaft running down the center surrounded by a hexagonal casing with a tiny spring on the end showing no visible signs of corrosion.

Experts date the geode-type rock to around *500,000 years ago* based on the time it would take for the fossil-encrusted nodule to form. Many believe the structure resembles a modern spark plug, but they're unable to explain its function or purpose, let alone how such a sophisticated device became wedged inside an ancient rock. Is this fossil the work of quantum physics? The Coso Artifact doesn't stand alone either.

Metallic oval tubes found in 1968, near Calvados, France, associatively date with their 65 million year old Cretaceous chalk encasing. According to the Universite de Caen, these tubes were formed by natural mineralization although they very much resemble something that might have been created using human intellect. Halfway around the world in Australia a similar artifact was discovered encased in coal by a foundry in 1885 known as the Salzburg cube. This precise metal cube found inside a block of coal proved to be manufactured with human ingenuity due to the sharp, perfectly straight edges. Skeptics believe the cube is nothing more than a slag piece of foundry equipment but the shear precision leads one to believe otherwise.

Coal often appears as a popular medium for unexplained or out of place embedded materials. One profound and well documented case refers to a ten inch, eight carat gold chain fused into the center of a piece of coal. An article in the 1891 Illinois Times explains how Mrs. S. W. Culp found a circular chain in a lump of coal which she broke apart to fit in a coal hod. Whereabouts of the gold chain are currently unknown. A very similar story happened a few years earlier in 1844, in Rutherford Mills, England.

Workers at the quarry uncovered a golden thread embedded in Carboniferous rock dating between 320 to 360 million years ago. Unfortunately the Rutherford case is not well documented for supporting evidence. In 1884, a nail embedded in an ancient sandstone block dating to the Mesozoic Era near Kingoodie in

Scotland again threw archeology for a loop.

Documentation on the case is solid except the report does not include the exact depth.

Then there is one of the most peculiar controversial discoveries to date. The London Hammer is referred to as a pre-flood artifact by the Bible Science Association and Creation Science Foundation. Due to the significance of the artifact to these organizations, it has not been thoroughly studied by an unbiased party in detail to provide accurate dating. In fact, the possessor, Carl Baugh, denied C14 dating on the object for many years, to which some believe may prove the date to be much more recent than pre-flood era.

Eventually he revealed results on the Internet of a C14 test claiming a date ranging from the present to around 1200 CE, although specific information regarding where the testing took place, or by who, was not disclosed. One theory suggests the hammer was dropped in a location where limestone sediment hardened to create a rock formation around it, and another theory claims the encased hammer had been fabricated in order to facilitate creationist motives.

Research conducted on the anomaly, the hammer's head revealed to be made from 96. 6% iron by weight, a feat only known to be possible by use of modern technology. Even if the hammer dates to a few hundred years ago, as an accepted common belief, it does not explain how the striking head is composed at such a level of purity. Scientific explanation purposes a lost or abandoned technology as responsible for casting the iron head.

Perhaps these mysterious objects found encased in ancient rocks share a common element in the quantum realm, or perhaps they are quite normal with logical explanations. For either case, these artifacts have not been deciphered to an acceptable level for everyone to understand. Are humans subconsciously capable of manifesting modern equipment or ideas into their past through quantum physics?

Lab studies in a double-slit experiment with lasers in 2007, France, proved that it's theoretically possible to change the past by manipulating laser detectors after an event occurred. This purposes more recent events may actually be results from future events manipulating the past. As perplexing and mind boggling as the quantum realm is, it challenges human perception to examine life outside of the box and further away from conditioned responses.

Quantum science explains that all objects do not come into human perception until they are observed, whereby the brain recognizes and interprets the object to exist once the object's light stimulates the optic nerve and visual cortex. If humans have a method of manipulating these energies on a conscious or subconscious level, then *theoretically it makes sense that they just might be able to manipulate the past, or the future for it is known, the capability of consciously changing the present.*

Energy Cycles

From birth to death of all living matter, life repeats itself in infinite cycles as life energy transforms from from one being to the next. Each loop slightly modifies the manifestation in ways which resemble the previous path. Evidence of these cycles is found in living creatures and inanimate objects alike. Organism survival instincts, behavioral traits, and identities are passed down from generation to generation, each with slight modifications from gene selection, primary survival mechanisms and ever-changing environmental influences.

Replications are similar yet unique to an organism's current existence at the same time. Environments face similar cycles in the birth and destruction of planets, orbital configurations, and material compositions. Lava from the sea floor spews forth into the ocean, eventually creating new land from the old. Water on the Earth evaporates into clouds above which condense and release moisture back unto the surface. Energy consistently proves it cannot be contained for too long before a recharge, or purification, is necessary for continuance. As energy exists throughout all matter, it is likewise for energy cycles.

Living organism food chains operate in a similar fashion from bacteria, phytoplankton, to small animals, and sizing upward to the top of the chain. When the particular chain's top dog comes to pass, the body decays and becomes nutrients which help start the cycle over again. Each tier during the process follows along an individual life cycle which by in part composes the master cycle. It is no coincidence the universe is made of billions upon billions of individual cycles.

Nature is very much known for its ability to achieve balance without interference from extremities. Although human impact on the environment may tell a different story at the moment, science claims planet Earth would recover very quickly if humanity faced extinction.

Where is the tipping point though, and just how far can cycles be pushed before the universe must realign those affected energies?

Deciphering the exact moment in which the universe requires borrowed energy to be returned seems like a near impossible task because the answer would technically be a prediction of death. Is there a ticking time block encoded into every living being's DNA which determines exactly when in the future it will be time to move on? Or could the moment be dependent on an energy spent versus energy recycled equilibrium?

For example, animal "A" intakes copious amounts of energy for long periods of time while the byproduct is transferred into slow-release elements causing a slight imbalance in consumption over return. At the same time, animal "B" intakes moderate amounts of energy with a moderate amount of byproduct in attempt to balance its impact on the environment. Then we have, animal "C" who lives on the most minimal amounts of energy and produces byproducts with the opposite effect as animal "A", coincidentally resulting in an imbalance in waste over consumption. If population and life expectancies in each scenario eventually even out, then nature is presented with an opportunity to balance energy without direct intervention.

Suppose animal "A" lifestyle results in a shorter life expectancy which ultimately drives "A"-type populations to the brink of extinction. This action creates a direct impact on "B" and "C" animals either extending their life expectancies or energy conversion efficiencies. A case in point, for example, are sea turtles with a very long life expectancy. Sea turtles may swim the oceans for a couple hundred years in an environment where buoyancy helps reduce energy exerted for energy intake. The turtles likely find sea buoyancy as advantageous for prolonging life with substantial opportunities for reproduction. Other animals in the oceans don't always follow suite to that of a reserved sea turtle.

Some animals may seem to be more active when compared to that of a turtle and spend their lives in a short conversion frenzy until death by reproduction, starting their cycle over again. If the short-living animal was an indirect source of food for the turtles and was driven to extinction (not by direct means of the turtle), the result may require sea turtles to change feeding habits, move elsewhere, and possibly develop a method in their energy recycling process to compensate for a lacking food source.

In the everyday hustle and bustle of modern life we sometimes forget about the perseverance of mother nature, the quick pace causes us to lose sight of nature's true intentions, what they really mean, and who we really are. Everything is part of the universe, be it an inanimate object or a living being – *We are all bound by the energy of the universe.* Part of something monumental beyond all available comprehension. Life is large, but the universe is much larger. Energy is the source of what is, and everything that will ever be. It flows through everything as a beautiful transmission of soft, comforting, vitality that defines the very significance of existing.

Energy seeks balance and union through both our thoughts and physical matter, it looks at the glass as both half full and half empty at the same time. When our minds are free from classifying what reality is, they too become free and limitless with no beginning or end as the true intention of life. Nature creates life in its image as an opportunity to experience the beauty of energy from an entirely different perspective, one that might not find otherwise by traversing the universe in another form. Planet Earth is a rest stop on the time-line of existence for souls to revitalize and recharge through inspiration, beauty, and love of nature in its purest sense. By borrowing energy to experience manifestation of life firsthand we are equipped with emotions capable of fortifying the heart and soul by bloom of nature.

Technology is undoubtedly changing the world on multiple levels. As the latest pride of human innovation, technology is designed to harness, control, and direct energy at the will of its manipulators. Although controlling energy has a beneficial side to the welfare of mankind, it is not without problems, and will one day succumb to mother nature regaining its almighty balance. Curing diseases, reducing health risks, improving life expectancy, and quality of nourishment are all positive benefits to the manipulation of energy by technology, but at what cost?

Damage to the environment has greatly increased since the industrial revolution along with the loss of several, now extinct, species of animals and plant life. Mortality rates for certain cancers appear to be declining but the overall number of incidences are rising. Psychological trauma, attention deficit disorder, drug abuse, and dyslexia plague recent generations of children as it seems increasingly acceptable to permit access to over-stimulating activities as technology becomes more commonplace. Life on Earth used to move at a much slower pace with a consistent conscious awareness of mankind's affect on the environment on a daily basis.

A large majority of our ancient ancestors, and a good portion of people around the world today, strongly believe we exist as part of nature, that we are not separated from it by any means, we are all interconnected. Our ancestors ritualistically gave praise to nature believing their gods were merely renditions of energy manifested in human-like forms; Their gods were not separate entities from nature and energy, a stark contrast when compared to modern idolatry beliefs. Ancient families did not attempt to exploit land or resources for profit, instead they took only what they needed in order to preserve balance in nature.

Life once revolved around a continuous respectful relationship with the environment for prosperity instead of clear-cutting rain forests to extract minerals. *We are an extension of nature and by destroying nature, we are destroying ourselves.* It is imperative to revisit those values passed down through the legacy of our ancestors, for the future survival humanity and the Earth, we must regain harmony in balance with nature. Living in a disposable society has turned the phrase "take only what you need" into "take all you can and throw away what you don't want" which is wreaking havoc on our environment and developing nations around the world.

Desert Rain

The Egyptians believed water is the source of all creation, to the point they often depicted those in the afterlife drinking from SHE, or a pool of water. Many motifs around Egypt also depict the SESEN (Lotus), an aquatic flower symbolizing birth and dawn as it rises from the water every morning and descends at night. Adapting to the harsh conditions of desert living could only prove successful if the culture was able to maintain an adequate supply of water.

Pyramids around the world share many common elements from an architectural standpoint as well as the use of megalithic blocks for their construction. Many rest in proximity to a fresh water source, something which humans cannot live without. Is it possible these gigantic structures provided much more for ancient civilizations than meets the eye?

The Great Pyramid of Giza, for example, does not contain hieroglyphs or artistic decorations inside yet archeology tells us the Egyptians built it as a tomb for Pharaoh Khufu. Why would the ancient Egyptians built such a large testament to a Pharaoh with only a few scattered inscriptions on the structure? Perhaps there is more to the mystery of the pyramids, and it might be a very simple explanation overlooked due to their complex nature.

Many alternative theories about the purpose of the pyramids have been suggested throughout the years. Physicists and geologists mention theories based on harnessing a currently unknown energy called subtle-energy. This energy is a result of the fluctuating magnetic field around Earth which tends to concentrate along Ley lines, and when these lines intersect, the energy concentration is at its highest. What if, perhaps, this is a partial answer to the question?

Several pyramids are thought to have been built along these Ley line intersection points and feature another important element in harnessing subtle-energy. Water residing below the Earth's surface – *"Min" according to the Egyptians*. Life ultimately depends on water for survival. It is a key ingredient in the chemical makeup of carbon-based lifeforms and is required as a vital part for the existence of life. Space explorations focus on finding water to find life, it's that critical to the scientific understanding of living, breathing organisms.

For many ancient civilizations, water is sacred. It is the fundamental element for ancient ritual, precious, and highly coveted. Suppose the Pyramid of Giza is a grand example of ancient man's efforts to ensure the most vital resource does not run out. Could the great pyramid actually be an ancient well, designed to move water from the Nile and below the Earth's surface, to a place closer to the Egyptians to prolong their survival while gaining valuable deposits of salt in the process?

There is evidence suggesting the great pyramid might actually be an ancient means for supplying water and salt to a very large population. When the core chamber rooms were originally uncovered, a layer of salt was discovered on the walls, the floor, and the ceiling. This alone suggests that mixed water from the Nile may have been stored or somehow pumped throughout. Until recent times, science believed the Nile river was not irrigated near the pyramid location due to the annual flood.

Years ago on an annual basis a new layer of soil was deposited and the Egyptians used it for growing crops. Nile water filtered through the soil, and as a result, water with a higher concentration of salt accumulated in the groundwater table. Extracting groundwater might have played an important role to ancient Egyptian culture as it provided not only water, but also a valuable salt resource, once evaporated, for use as currency and in preservation. As for extracting the salts from the water, maybe the Egyptians had a unique way of doing this. What if the Dendera Light bulb found at the Temple of Hathor isn't really a light bulb, but instead a giant desalination device with a depiction of the sacred blue Lotus as a reference to water inside the tube?

Chambers inside the pyramid are constructed from granite which is capable of ionizing the air and emitting radon. To this day, the blocks are still so finely placed together that even a thin piece of paper or razor blade cannot be placed between them. Mortar-free construction with gigantic megalithic blocks is one way of preserving a structure for thousands of years by little maintenance, but it is also useful in the sense that it provides a natural seal, preventing water from flowing between the blocks – *What a great way to store water in ancient times!* Granite is a poor thermal conductor, in turn providing another benefit considering heat accelerates decay by the release of silica and potassium ions when granite is exposed to water over long periods of time.

The shafts running from what is known as the King's and Queen's chambers align to Orion's Belt, Sirius, Alpha Draco, and Kochab, but they may also have an alternate purpose when compared to modern theories.

Deep below Giza is an area called The Pit which features two passageways. One from near the groundwater table to the ascending passage on a low inclined angle, and a smaller shortcut route running almost vertical, deemed an air vent which connects the ascending passage to the Grand Gallery.

The Pit extends by two small shafts in the opposite directions, one straight down to the water table, and one directly opposite of the ascending passage toward the Nile river – *Is this one of Herodotus' fabled underground water canals?*

Suppose this configuration was specifically designed to move water from the ground table using hydraulics, up the passageways into the two chambers and up the air shafts? Leftover salt as water evaporated in the desert heat could be collected as water channeled to the plateau and fields for irrigation.

Evidence also points to the outside of Giza once finished in a white limestone coating, a material much more susceptible to erosion than the inside granite core. The benefit of using this type of coating is that it's an excellent insulator to protect the core from unwanted heat in the system. At the same time, this combination helps minimize natural evaporation inside the pyramid and reduce accelerated bacteria growth found in warmer waters, especially in non-aerated water systems.

One crucial aspect to the water well theory is known evidence of water erosion in the area around and on the Great Sphinx. The subject remains a controversial subject due to the fact historians have pieced together a story of Egypt based on ancient artifacts and hieroglyphs found throughout all of Egypt; yet the story does not jive with natural processes theorized to occur in the area over thousands of years. According to geologists, area geomorphology, and GPR studies, erosion on the Sphinx and The Pit walls demonstrates a very clear pattern distinctly characteristic of wear and tear from repeated exposure to water or rain, not just wind or sand storms.

Climatologists know the Nile valley was once a lush tropical paradise over 10,000 years ago before it dried up to become the Sahara known today. Area geology and erosion evidence due to rain means Egypt's beloved Sphinx is much older than historical record indicates. Perhaps ancient Egyptians inherited the inspirational monument, or maybe it was built by much older Egyptians who's written record became lost in the sands of times. At the moment science does not have a marking identifying an exact date the

Sphinx was constructed or when it was completed, it must use associative dating techniques along with results of geological conditions over time.

There is a way, though, where the historical record could sync with the evidence of water erosion on the Sphinx and in The Pit. Due to land topology, the flooding Nile could not be the culprit even if river flow is traced back thousands of years. Rainfall is the likely catalyst, but that too falls into the similar situation of back-dating the Sphinx beyond the time of Pharaoh Khafra. According to climatology, Min (the rain god) was not very busy at all during the period, producing on average one inch of rain per year – *Why have a rain god in an area of the world with little to no rain at all?*

If the Pyramids were once used for extracting water and salt, or as part of the process, maybe the Sphinx was part of the same vitality system. Again looking at topology, the Sphinx rests below the elevation of the pyramids allowing gravity to naturally carry water towards it. Did the pit area serve as a water reservoir to nourish ancient Egyptians? Did the purposed pyramid wells spring a leak at one point, flooding toward the Sphinx for many years before it was repaired? Was the Sphinx used for any type of ritual process involving water?

Another important piece of information is the term, river delta, which originally obtained its meaning by the triangular delta-shaped network of rivers emptying the Nile river into the Mediterranean Sea, the very same delta shape of the pyramids.

Greek historian Herodotus described a series of great waterways as an underground drainage system below the Giza plateau. In modern times, archaeologists find a notched entrance which some believe to be proof of Giza's construction as a gateway to a series of ramps spiraling inward, possibly designed to push heavy granite blocks on sledges to the top. This unique design may point toward evidence of a water propelled device such as a paddle mill or cart system that moves along the grooved cut-outs on either side of the hallway. Due to the natural slope in the area, water run-off from the hydraulic construction could account for the strange erosion found nearby on the Pit walls and on the Sphinx.

Archaeologists believe granite used in the construction was moved from the Aswan quarry, approximately 500 miles away, using the Nile river to float giant blocks on vessels downstream. They Egyptians were well aware of water's buoyant ability to move heavy objects using floating wooden structures.

Herodotus claims at least ten years of preparation was spent on the pyramid grounds, waterways, ramps, and underground chambers prior to construction. Perhaps water might have been used in the construction itself. When the larger granite blocks are in place and sealed, the chambers could be filled with water to float blocks on wooden vessels to the next level; Sealing off the next chamber, filling it with water and repeating the process until the top is reached.

After the pyramid was built, water inside could be released simply by carefully unblocking the main entrance or part of the underground tunnel system. Using water to build pyramids is surely a unique approach to the puzzle and it may not apply to all large block pyramid builds. Yet it might explain why some of the earlier pyramids faced structural problems if they also had to account for the weight and distribution of water inside.

Above all, pyramids in Egypt became the ultimate tombs for pharaohs, tracing the skyline in symbolism of the afterlife and the creation of man. As the last thousands of years, Egypt's pyramids will continue to fill onlookers with awe and inspiration that monumental achievements *can be accomplished* by dedicated efforts of an entire civilization.

J.C. Vintner

Collective Consciousness

Scientific research is trending away from attempts to answer questions about the bigger picture. The universe is so unimaginably large, and with this observation it's proving to be a daunting task to explain events occurring in our own galaxy, let alone the vast quantity of space beyond. Instead, research focus is shifting inward, into the spiritual realm, with specific attention to our conscious being. Our private inner thought process is a key element to defining us as human.

The mind's ability to manipulate matter inside the brain for data retention and regurgitation is very mysterious. Imagine if science was able to unlock the full potential of the human mind. Perhaps traveling to the distant reaches of the universe might not be so far away. If communication between two humans can be carried out successfully on Earth, who's to say it's not possible to communicate to the distant reaches of our galaxy and even the universe?

Telepathic studies in Mexico have demonstrated what appears to be a subconscious link, in the form of a brain wave pattern, between two isolated subjects. This documented event highly suggests an ability exists for humans to communicate with each other using only their minds. These results agree with a quantum prediction by Dr. Amit Goswami, a very well known Theoretical Quantum Physicist, which refers to particle measurements of correlated brains. Amit insists that consciousness maintains the correlation. His research is part of a scientific movement toward explaining human consciousness and understanding the strange world of PSI phenomena.

Quantum thinking may explain other phenomena such as remote viewing. Several countries world-wide have admitted at the government level of using remote viewing techniques for both reconnaissance and game theory, to astonishing accuracy.

If humans are currently able to tap into a global conscious for means of data retrieval and communication, then perhaps the question of the existence of telepathy has already been answered. Explaining such phenomena at the scientific level might become problematic on several levels other than the science itself.

Governments interested in protecting remote viewing programs may find it necessary to silence information that might expose the program or provide competing governments with the opportunity to run similar programs. Implications of a very successful remote viewing program by any government could have profound and devastating effects on the world even if they change perception of how the universe works.

Remote viewing isn't the only tried, tested, and true government funded research field using extra sensory perception for thought projections and data retrieval. Some medical studies centered around brain activity and function have developed machines capable of reading brain waves and interpreting the results to create physical actions. This type of technology is attempting to utilize parts of the brain to perform tasks by isolating thoughts before or as they're happening.

The Neuroengineering Center at Duke University designed a space allowing monkeys to move an avatar to identify virtual objects using only their brain activity. Several psycho-kinetic studies are participating in a race to create wearable devices capable of moving objects with brain waves. This type of research is heavily fueled by the growing desire to restore degraded muscle functions and bypass broken nerve connections in paralyzed individuals. Until recently, Psychokinesis was demonstrated via mainstream media by bending objects with the mind such as a spoon, or by levitating a subject in a magic show.

Break-through field studies are edging science closer to creating a fully functional end-user device capable of moving physical objects with only a human mind. Moving or manipulating objects with only the mind by aid of technology. As the technology advances it might one day enable us to perform wireless, that is, if ESP and psycho-kinetic research doesn't find a way first.

True mind over matter without an aid, it can't be too far away. Psycho-kinetic, Telekinetic, and Parapsychology studies are continuing to build up concrete evidence that humans indeed possess a type of spiritual connection, be it with each other, another dimension, or distant places around the universe.

Anything is possible with the right mindset. Remote viewing experts call it an underlying phenomena that anyone can access as they perfect the art.

Enough research demonstrates something peculiar is there, but not enough to satisfy all skeptics. Perhaps the time may come when humans rediscover a missing spiritual link in the mind. A link which was long forgotten over many thousands of years, allowing telepathy with others, the planet, animals, and the universe. At that moment it will be imperative for every spiritual mind across Earth's surface to meditate and channel together as one collective consciousness, to let the universe know ability has returned – *Beyond anything technology can tell us, we are all part of nature.*

Cause and Effect

Everyone has heard the phrase at least once in their life, what goes around comes around, and for good reason. As we learn more about ancient teachings, the more evident it becomes that the law of cause and effect is a powerful yet unwritten subtle connection between all things in the known universe. Choose to ignore it and life might become frustrating on a daily basis. The bible speaks of cause and effect on several levels, but it's probably the most well known excerpt that really hits home, treat others how you would like to be treated.

In a simplified way this statement beckons for good to be done to receive good in return. There's also an unwritten rule about the unwritten rule; Mainly that cause and effect seeks pure and sincere goodness without selfish or malicious intent. What is good to some, may not be so great to others, and according to theologists, the universe governs every transfer of good and evil instantaneously even-though an effect might be delayed from its impact.

Since the universe must maintain its order, all effects require the universe to rearrange itself on a complex level in a very dynamic system. This process eliminates the possibility of life becoming too unbalanced for forward momentum.

The epic story of Buddha demonstrates extreme spiritual aptitude in the quest for awakening and enlightenment. Despite the fact that Buddha was raised in privilege with the finest quality clothes, shelter and food fit for a king, he sought to find an end to suffering and fear at any cost. This pilgrimage started with a feeling of disillusion between life in lavish palaces and the outside world. After finally seeing the world outside of the palace, he questioned how he was to enjoy a life of pleasure when the world is in suffering.

At first the Buddha believed an answer could be found as a wandering monk. In torn robes he traveled from place to place studying the teachings of wise men and philosophers yet still could not find an answer to the question. Next, the Buddha spent six years practicing asceticism believing it would bring him to enlightenment only to realize that pushing himself to the brink of death could not possibly lead to happiness. Finally he sat beneath a Bodhi tree meditating and claiming that he would not leave the spot until he found an answer to end suffering. Here the Buddha was tempted to stray from the path to enlightenment by lustful desires, lightning storms and demonic armies. He resisted every temptation while defeating evils opposing him. The Buddha was spiritually awakened from the experience and realized how to end suffering.

Teachings of Buddha fundamentally begin with three universal truths discovered along the path to enlightenment. The first states matter turns into energy and energy turns into matter. Given this principal concept he claims humans are the same as other humans, plants, trees, and the Earth. Just as life is a physical manifestation of energy, it is the same truth everywhere energy exists. The second universal truth states everything is continuously changing at variable rates. Sometimes changes are very slow and go unnoticed while in other times they move quickly and create a substantial amount of noise.

As human consciousness evolves we becomes increasingly aware of new methods for achieving goals to reach spiritual destinations. Since human consciousness continues to change, so must everything it perceives. The final universal truth taught by Buddha is the law of cause and effect, more commonly known as Karma. Planting positive seeds to enjoy positive fruits and prosperity. Projecting good thoughts and actions ensures future good thoughts and actions will happen in return. This concept puts human consciousness in control of its destiny whereby thoughts and actions of an individual are returned at a future time, good or bad.

To end suffering is to harness will power to extinguish ignorance and greed while abiding by the law of cause and effect. Everyone eventually falls victim to suffering in one way or another, at no fault of their own, by law of nature. Old age, the loss of loved ones, and sickness are common catalysts to emotional suffering. These ailments are often responsible for ignorance of karma and create a contagious trend which spreads throughout the world as wildfire. Dousing society's modern wildfire may present itself as a near impossible task given the many thousands of years evil and ignorance have rampaged the lands. Just as suffering finds ways to infiltrate consciousness, mankind can find ways to alleviate the burden.

Seven billion minds together in peaceful meditation may unlock secrets of the universe which were previously unimaginable to exist. A massive global shift in focus from psychological albatross to conscientious blessings may finally bring the world to peace. Emotion is a human interpretation of received energy. The idea of a peaceful planet is eventually realized by every soul searcher on Earth, and....

Even if it remains on the tip of the mind's tongue for years, is rooted deep in the heart's desire to enjoy a peaceful life.

Electromagnetic Fields

The Earth is nestled inside a constantly changing magnetic field which fluctuates in result of inner core processes. Coincidentally this magnetic field protects the surface from high levels of radiation emanating from the sun, thus contributing to the unique conditions supporting life on the planet.

Paleomagnetists understand Earth's magnetic field swaps poles (or reversals) roughly every hundred thousand years by evidence discovered in rock layers throughout the world. These alterations to ancient rocks eerily prove the ability of a strong magnetic field and its influence on physical matter. This evidence is how geologists are aware of Earth's polar shift phases every 50,000 years like clockwork.

It took until middle ages for creditable documents to surface with an applicable understanding of magnetism by aiding ship navigation with a compass. Before then, written documents about electricity and magnetism are few and far between, but it's apparent our ancestors had a basic understanding by artifacts discovered from ancient Olmec and Chinese cultures. There's also an intriguing device discovered in Mesopotamia dating to a short period between 200-600 BCE called the Bagdad Battery, seemingly designed to extract an electric charge from chemical reactions using acidic solutions.

Dating back even further is a strange depiction, referred to as the Dendera light bulb, carved into an ancient Egyptian hieroglyphic relief found inside the Temple of Hathor; Historians claim the tube-like structure is actually a rendition of a lotus flower. Another ancient culture with a potential understanding of electricity and magnetic fields is the Mayans. The Pyramid of the Sun (Mica Temple) in Teotihuacan featured several layers of deliberately placed mica sheets under large block floors until much of it was sold off by the first archaeologists exploring the temple. Though it is not clear what the intended use of mica was, we know it has a variety of modern industrial uses including electrical component insulation.

Paranormal investigators have discovered and related certain unexplained experiences as a link between sightings of apparitions and concentrated electromagnetic fields. The human brain houses a neural network capable of transmitting information using electricity which in turn creates an electric field. To some, this electric field is an aura of energy susceptible to changing environmental conditions and interactions with other auras.

Electromagnetic fields are viewed as a continuous structure by a combination of a magnetic field and an electric field. Studies involving a magnet attached to a pair of glasses and placed in the center of a person's forehead for several days resulted in an unexplained type of magnetic hallucination where the subject believed they were seeing ghosts and shadowy figures. A phenomena known as a fear cage is often reported in areas where the EMF is very strong, usually in locations with exposed high voltage power lines, microwaves, and high radio frequencies.

Effects from fear cages sound eerily like a television drug commercial. They can include paranoia, moderate to severe disorientation, dizziness, depression and pains or aches in strange locations, all of which contribute toward the notion of paranormal activity manifested during an event. Strong electromagnetic fields indicate tend to indicate the presence of an apparition if no known human cause can be found according to ghost hunters.

Traditional ghost hunting relying on an EMF meter often suggests stronger fields as short-lived while moving throughout the environment. Likely the fields could be affecting the human brain just long enough to alter its electromechanical properties, in turn causing a sort of hallucinatory response, but studies at high EMF levels have not been sanctioned anywhere in the world due to inherent risk.

A magnetic field is created when electrons are aligned in the same direction, enabling an object the ability to attract or repel objects with magnetic properties. Science does not understand why or exactly how particles generate fields at the structural level. Although quantum mechanics can theoretically describe particles and their behaviors, it doesn't provide a clear answer to what magnetism is or why it exists. Could it be possible that particles have properties beyond those discussed through quantum mechanics?

Aligning several electrons will create a positive or negative magnetic field relative to the orientation of particles. An electron in motion generates a small magnetic field which extends in all directions infinitely, so maybe when two electrons are brought close together the magnetic fields superimpose, increasing the tiny magnetic field's strength also by two. Thus, once several electrons are placed together along the same orientation, the whole magnetic field of an object becomes as strong as a product of the combination of magnetic fields surrounding electrons in the system. How magnetism truly works at the atomic level may remain a mystery for years to come, but it's impact on daily life will always be certainly profound to say the least.

One of the oldest references to a possible magnetic device dates to around 2,600 BCE during the Chinese Hoang-ti dynasty with a chariot carrying a female figurine, who divided the world into four parts, and always managed to point South no matter the orientation of the chariot. The Olmec civilization is also believed to be another ancient culture with knowledge of magnetic properties, gathered by studying Monte Alto carvings, and "Fat Boy" sculptures in Guatemala. Each unique statue has magnetic poles aligned with the figure's temples, navel, and ears. These features strongly indicate a knowledge of magnetic properties to incorporate the right materials in multiple carvings ritualistically.

Magnetic history doesn't stop here either. Ancient Maya and Indian cultures also dabbled in magnetic stone sculpting. Ancient Greek texts tell us the Egyptians used magnetism commonly, including for building purposes. Since natural magnets can be located almost anywhere in the world and it's not entirely surprising that ancient cultures found curiosity in strange attracting rocks. The modern marvel of Coral Castle also points toward electromagnetic influence of another kind, one that possibly the Egyptians were using to build the pyramids according to Ed Leedskalnin – *His manuscript puts emphasis on the knowledge of a key to the universe as a unique electromagnetic coupling.*

When examining monumental ancient structures around the world we find intricate wave pattern relief carvings thought by scientists to resemble electromagnetic radio spectrum field waves, acoustic sound waves, water waves, or snake-like animals. Without direct texts describing the wave pattern's purpose, a logical answer always points to water, as the vital source of life and part of the four primary elements, it's importance is very significant to ancient cultures. Snake motifs tend to fit very well in translation here too as their locomotion is commonly observed in wave patterns.

Another important point focuses on the fact that we've only uncovered a small fraction of knowledge about our ancestors – *It's difficult to assume waves mean water unless we have detailed language telling us specifically.* We know our distant relatives were capable of monumental feats at a nearly incomprehensible scale; Electromagnetism could be the critical unknown piece to the puzzle required to understand the knowledge of our ancient ancestors.

J.C. Vintner

Time Travel

One of the most interesting yet difficult to understand concepts of quantum physics involves time travel. Science fiction often portrays traveling to the future and past by aid of a machine simplified so much that all the traveler needs to do is punch in a destination date and hit a button. Logistic problems plague the possibility of travel along the fourth dimension. There is the grandfather paradox. If a person traveled to the past and prevented their grandfather from meeting their grandmother would they still exist?

Currently science entertains three theories suggesting ways nature would compensate and prevent paradoxes from occurring if time travel became possible. First, traveling back into time would put the traveler into a parallel dimension which looks and feels exactly as the dimension they traveled from, but any interactions which would change the course of history happen in the alternate dimension with absolutely no effect on the source dimension.

The second theory puts the time traveler into an observation only mode whereby they only exist in the past in spirit with no possible way to alter the past. Interestingly enough this sounds very familiar in certain paranormal investigations with apparitions suspected as time travelers from the past or future manifesting with ghost-like figures. The last theory presents a unique situation which states that any alteration to the past will cause the space time fabric to change in order to rearrange time to the point it was before the alteration happened.

In other words, if a time traveler tried to change the past, the past would find a way to correct the change and prevent a paradox. Thus anyone traveling back in time could try to change history but anything they do in the past will not affect the present or future even by the slightest change. Physics is governed by the laws of nature and to this date science has not once found a way in which nature would allow a paradox to exist.

However, many scientists now believe the concept of time travel into the future is theoretically plausible because skipping forward into time will not create paradoxes. Stephen Hawking addressed the issue with respect to research by Albert Einstein and the basic laws of how time works. Einstein demonstrated that mass creates a drag on the space-time continuum. The more mass, the greater it slows relative time. Hawking pointed out scientific evidence of mass affecting time by referring to the global positioning satellite system. Each of the 31 GPS satellites have a very precise atomic clock for measuring their location in space relative to time, and those clocks need to make constant adjustments on a daily basis to stay in sync with clocks on Earth running slightly slower.

Given this evidence, Hawking believes it is possible to travel into the future. He presumes that by sending a spacecraft to orbit the massive black hole in the center of the Milky Way, anyone on board would age at least half as fast as those on Earth during the same time period, due to the black hole's gigantic mass dragging on time. Stephen also suggests a less dangerous approach to travel into the future by simply traveling as close to the speed of light as possible for a set period of time.

Physics laws depend on light traveling at a constant velocity anywhere in the universe and that its speed cannot be surpassed. Theory states at the moment anything becomes close to exceeding the speed of light, time itself will slow it down to maintain the constant law. Meaning that if an object was traveling close to the speed of light with passengers on board, and one of the passengers tries to run forward, time will slow the passenger down to ensure they are not exceeding the constant.

Hawking's theory of traveling into the future may have a vital flaw though. Just as he describes travel to the past to be impossible due to the creation of paradoxes, traveling to the future may create paradoxes of their own too. The basis of this theory is called the future-self paradox. Suppose a time traveler seeking to alter the past, by preventing his grandfather from meeting his grandmother, instead traveled to the future to prevent his own death. The paradox shifts from eliminating himself from existence to a continuation of existence by repeating this action – *Both sides must be looked at in the same light.*

Traveling to the future using a large mass such as a black hole to drag on time is only affecting anyone close to the large mass and those further away continue to age at a time relative to their location. Hence, those in the craft are not seeing the future as originally cogitated by science fiction enthusiasts.

In essence the purpose of Sci-Fi time travel is to provide humanity with a means of altering the past and changing the future, or using information from the future to change the present. To prevent disasters before they happen and to positively change lives.

Unfortunately if traveling to either the past or the future became possible, then the world would become an entirely different place.

Presume the big bang wasn't really a big bang at all, but instead imagine our universe was created from a very different origin not yet thoroughly explored by science – *A black hole.*

What science does know about black holes is very limited and in fact it's probably really close to the same amount of knowledge about the origin of the universe. It's quite possible the big bang wasn't such a chaotic event spewing particles randomly in all directions, maybe our universe was pushed through a black hole 13.7 billion years ago, the very same way funnel clouds and water spouts work on Earth. We don't really know what goes on inside one although we're aware of certain observed properties.

Black holes bend light which makes it seem to disappear, and they're assumed to rip apart matter, and maintain a very dense mass quite possibly related to the sum of material swallowed by the vortex. According to the Law of Conservation of Energy, energy cannot be created or destroyed, which means a black hole to abiding by this law can only shift energy from one form into another, and not destroy it. What if black holes are space-cyclone access points to alternate realms in a Matryoshka universe.

Moving particles through the black hole to another attached layer works just like a wormhole is believed to be a shortcut in time.

Currently, there is a way for anyone to travel in time in the virtual sense, by accessing the human mind to recall past events. Depending entirely upon the individual, recalled events may be remembered in bits and pieces or become skewed while lacking sufficient detail. Since our brains use retained memories in order to access past information, the data is susceptible to influence of imagination.

Unfortunately fine details of events are sometimes easily forgotten although such controversial practices like hypnosis have been able to successfully recover vital information. Since we are capable of all or part of actual events in our past by using the mind's eye, perhaps there is way to access the past using technology developed to read retained memories.

Maybe thoughts exist in their true reality through another dimension or perhaps as an accessible universe. Quantum mechanics suggests the existence of multiple universes and how mankind may be able to access these realms in the not too distant future. Usually these scenarios are played out with great advances in technology, super computers, and complex machines.

Perhaps exploration in the quantum universe begins with the Cerebral Cortex which already allows us to travel into the past and imagine the future. Modern record keeping technologies are enhancing the way we recall our past by providing indisputable evidence of past events in the form of photographs, videos, and sound recordings. Ground breaking research in the areas of clairvoyance and remote viewing is steadily opening a door enabling people a theoretical means of predicting the future.

Remote viewing by extra sensory perception became well known to the general public in the 1970's when the United States funded a research program after discovering Russia and China were running ESP programs. Government agencies such as the FBI and CIA also utilize ESP type abilities for forensics, profiling, and psychic detectives. The military practices a similar form, although highly based on mathematics, through a brilliant concept called game theory attempts to predict possible outcomes of war tactics in order to develop effective war game strategies.

Government agencies seek solutions to complex dilemmas quickly and efficiently. Spending less time, money, or effort to solve problems leaves excess spending dollars which in turn can be appropriated elsewhere such as intelligence research and development programs. Always being one step ahead helps task forces prevent situations from getting out of hand and harming more innocent civilians.

ESP, however, is not a new concept born in the 20th century. Visions from 16th century Nostradamus still captivate and intrigue curiosity of the masses. Historians tell us Nostradamus walked a fine line along the Church's belief system while he dabbled in alchemy, astrology, and often participated in ritualistic practices designed to induce foresight visions.

Michel Nostradamus' prophecies seem to follow a pattern suggested to repeat in history. His quatrains continuously manage to awe and inspire those who believe there's a little more to life than meets the eye while continuously referring to events in the current timescale. It's as though Michel's quatrains are balanced with the perfect amount of obscurity designed to allow imagination to run rampant to find answers.

Passages found throughout the Bible also speak of prophecy, they also fit along a similar pattern in the sense that Biblical prophecies always seem to be on the verge of fulfillment. Scholars believe the interpretation of ancient prophecy requires a delicate touch. Seeking correlations between the present and what might happen in the future can be easily influenced by knowledge of the past. The idea of prophecy has transcended generations for thousands of years and some believe it dates back beyond the creation of written language. Prophecies traditionally link divine beings providing a foreseer with visions of the future, and to some this is a type of extra sensory perception, a sixth sense.

Prophecy does not at all seem out of the ordinary. Evolution and archeology explains that thousands of years ago mankind transitioned from a survival hunter-gatherer stance to an agricultural culture. As man first began to cultivate crops they looked toward the heavens for ways of predicting when to plant, when to harvest, when to pick, and when to migrate. Our ancestors knew seasons were changing, they realized how important it was to learn how to accurately forecast those changes for increased yields and seasonal preparations.

Using star positions along with phases of the moon and sun gave way to a revolutionary new method of predicting the future for survival. At some point, someone back then must have wondered if the same concept applied to people as the seasons of Earth. Could human actions be predicted in preparation for confrontation in the future and how would those predictions remain protected from abuse?

J.C. Vintner

Psychics & Superstitions

The belief of a broken mirror resulting in seven years of bad luck is most likely one of the most well known superstitions in the world. Just hearing the phrase makes anyone take a little extra care while moving and hanging mirrors. For many thousands of years people relied on highly polished metals as a reflective surface which held multiple purposes in daily life such as applying makeup, redirecting light, or even starting fires by focusing light into a fine point.

When the Romans created easier to break glass mirrors with a thin metal backing, mirror superstitions really went into overdrive. Cultures during the period considered any images seen in mirrors otherworldly and believed those images represented souls captured in another realm or dimension. If the mirror broke while someone was looking into it, the soul became trapped in many pieces, requiring either every single piece of the mirror to be ground into a fine dust or face seven years of bad luck while allowing the soul to mend. A soul is a direct reflection of who a person is; It's the light within and an energy binding life to their existence. What's very interesting about mirrors and bad luck stories is how believers refer to the soul becoming trapped inside another realm or dimension, almost alluding to a specific method for interacting or communicating with an alternate dimension. If it's true, that a broken mirror with a captured soul really does affect its reflective world physically, then it makes sense to have some sort of existing dimensional connection in order this to happen.

Although it's more likely that superstitions are created based on psychological conditioning, where subconscious affects conscious behavior over time, the idea of connecting to another dimension with something as simple as a mirror is difficult to ignore. Superstitions are known to instill concern because they thrive by fear, an emotion most people like to avoid for good reason. Yet the act of warding fear repetitively using trinkets, following old wives tales, and performing acts to expel evil spirits still seems to eerily reassemble a conditioned response similar to Pavlov's law.

Each time the act is successful, or seems successful, it teaches the mind subconsciously to expect a certain type of response in the future. Behavioral psychologists refer to the brain acting in this manor as associative learning, a theory in which all things a person has learned stem from a seeded thought. If the current state is an amalgamation of everything ever learned in the history of humanity, then it's perfectly normal for anyone to be afraid of what the future might hold through its unpredictable nature.

Perhaps uncertainty of the future is exactly what makes it so appealing to curiosity. Foreseeing the future has long been a desired reality among many people worldwide with a slew of practiced psychic mediums striving to make it happen. Our ancestors sought ways to foretell future events, and determine their place in the universe, because they understood of deep connections between everything that exists, that together those connections provide access to a universal knowledge capable of changing life as we know it.

Predicting the future accurately can change one's destiny for better or for worse.

Perhaps part of the difficulty in achieving a tried and tested method for deciphering what the future holds is due to the laws of physics. Altering the future or past from the present has the potential to create a paradox which, according to quantum law, could not happen. This means most likely, through entanglement, the universe would correct itself to compensate for the change in the predestined outcome.

The presence of true psychic individuals either means spirituality and the soul does not abide by the laws of physics, suggesting there's a way of learning both the past and future without consequence, or that laws of physics are incomplete and lack sufficient theories to apply to the human spirit.

Numerology is a unique method of mathematics designed for reducing events, names, places and more, down to single digit numbers which are believed to each have its own significant meaning or prediction. For example, if someone's birthday was 01/21/1911, it would be written in numerology as 0+1+2+1+1+9+1+1 equaling 16, or 1+6, for a final result of the number seven. The result is then cross referenced as the *number 7,* being the searcher and seeker of truth for understanding.

With a little research we find there are several and more elaborate explanations for each number all depending on the discipline involved. Using numbers in this fashion presents similar life predictions as Tarot Readings, Palm Readings, Crystal Balls, and Astrology.

Belief in psychic prediction is often an awkward pill to swallow for many people but there are quite a few world renown psychics working to alter this perspective, even if not by intention. Psychics are heavily scrutinized for a presumed ability to tap into PSI energy interconnecting all living beings, and the dead, in order to predict the future and provide recollection of past events, yet there are government agencies such as the FBI and CIA who employ specialized psychics for criminal investigations. Success reported by these agencies indicates the existence of a very true unexplainable phenomena capable of saving lives.

The legacy of Edgar Cayce touched the lives of thousands of people by making accurate predictions. Known as the Sleeping Prophet, Edgar would enter a trance-like sleep and answer questions asked to him during the slumber. Questions were given to a transcriber who took them directly to Cayce for answers, he would not meet with anyone face to face, ensuring any predictions would not be influenced by physical impression. The sheer number of accurate predictions dedicated Edgar a place in history along with the preservation of his living quarters.

Significance of 3

How is the third number respected in ancient belief systems, and how does understanding its meaning help us to unlock some of the greatest mysteries known to mankind, as through the third eye?

Concepts of the number 3 and its meaning to ancient people are reminiscent of an earlier research effort conducted several years ago involving the number 7's relationship to spirituality. The thought-provoking questions presented by ancient alien theorists managed to rekindle its prominence and suggest the idea of an even deeper understanding. These two numbers meet up on several mysterious levels when exploring scientific and religious realms of our history.

A question proposed by ancient mystery theorists asks in relation to the number 3, why it is the three Biblical Magi (wise-men) chose to bring Gold, Frankincense and Myrrh as gifts to baby Jesus. They followed the Star of Bethlehem as a guiding light from the heavens to find him.

One note here which is not normally mentioned in relation: The arrival of the Magi is still celebrated today by some Western Christians, on Three Kings' Day, the Epiphany, or the Twelfth Day as it's believed the event occurred 12 days after Christmas. Eastern traditions claim there were actually 12 Magi, instead of three who visited Jesus. In either case, twelve days or twelve Magi using numerology may be written as 1+2, or again, three.

Mentioning of the star is important from a spiritual perspective, but it also helps pin-point the exact birth of Jesus according to Biblical scholar, Simo Parpola. By his astronomical calculations, Parpola is able to show the triple conjunction of Saturn and Jupiter, occurred three times in the year 7 BC, as Saturn and Jupiter were in the constellation Pisces in close conjunction during the time of December 23, recorded on a Babylonian clay tablet.

Parpola's research primarily focuses on the actual date of Jesus' birth by means of archaeological evidence and astronomical data, reasoning the triple conjunction as the only possible explanation of the Star of Bethlehem from an astrological standpoint. The same triple conjunction alignment was observed twice since 7 BC, as Parpola explains, occurring every 800 years; marking 2,383 as the next year it may be witnessed.

Pisces is the twelfth (1+2 = 3) sign of the Zodiac and is represented also using 3 lines, 1 straight and 2 curved.

Perhaps the most intriguing relationship between the number 3 and the number 7 is presented to us when examining at least 3 written languages, Greek Γ, and Arabic ٣, and Urdu ٣. Written forms of the digit 3 appear graphically similar as a reversed number 7, which all are believed to stem from Gimel, the third letter in ancient Phoenician and Aramaic writing systems. Asking ourselves how the number 3 could unlock unexplained mysteries in mankind's distant past is a question met with certain difficulties; especially considering how closely numbers factor into our everyday lives.

Hollow Earth

Suppose the Earth, and other planets throughout the universe, have hollow cores instead of previously theorized molten rock and metal. This concept focuses around entrance points at the magnetic poles along with alternative entrance routes, back doors if you will, accessible from various points on the Earth's surface including entryways below the Great Pyramid, Mayan ruins, and more.

Science theorizes the Earth's core is actually liquid magma based on seismic wave density research, and that in order for the planet's magnetic field to exist, the core must be liquid state metal at high pressures.

The closest suggestion to any type of void in the center of the Earth is a light element, presumably oxygen or sulfur, composing around ten percent of the mass according to Geophysicists. Pointing a finger at the Earth's core may not necessarily provide accurate disprovable evidence of Hollow Earth theory in the sense that claimants could be referring to a hollow area somewhere between the 1,800 miles from Earth's crust to the outer core.

The problem, however, are theorized estimates of average temperatures ranging from 1,000 to 3,700 degrees Celsius due to conductive heat transfer from the liquid center.

Cavern systems found throughout the world support the idea of hollow structures residing below the Earth's surface, but due to the increasing temperature the deeper you go, the safe habitable zone falls near ~1. 16 miles (1867 meter) deep where temperatures average around 90 degrees Fahrenheit in non-geothermal active areas. Part of scientific theory has been proven already in the world's deepest mines, located in South Africa, reaching in excess of 3,500 meters with hopes of reaching the 5,000 meter mark in the future.

In these mining areas special cooling equipment is required to combat temperatures upward of 70 degrees Celsius and miners also deal with increased pressures capable of causing rocks to sometimes explode as they're lifted to lower pressure areas. The Earth's geological composition makes it difficult to entertain the idea of a hollow Earth, let alone life other than microbes thriving at such temperatures, but it does not rule out the possibility of vast hollows occupying the safe zone within the crust. The world's deepest known cave, Krubera, has been successfully explored up to a depth of nearly 2,200 meters. Close competitors include Cehi 2, Sima de la Cornisa, Pantjukhina, Sarma, Torca del Cerro, Jean Bernard, Vogelshacht, Gouffre Mirolda, and Mezhonnogo, all range from 1,500 to over 1,700 meters deep.

It's theoretically possible, though unlikely by modern science, given the porous nature of the Earth's crust that an unknown or alien civilization could inhabit the safe zone or below with specialized high tech equipment. There are a substantial number of known access points by cavern systems and likely a greater number of undiscovered caves which could permit hollowed underground areas for living. Exploring these areas has only become feasible due to recent advances in technology and due to that fact it might be too early to tell until further evidence is uncovered.

We have legends and structural evidence suggesting people may have lived underground at one point in Earth's history. Consider the huge underground ancient city of Derinkuyu in Turkey with enough room to safely accommodate 2,000 to 3,000 people along with food stores and livestock.

Even though archaeologists believe the city dates to around the 8th century BCE, it features advanced engineering techniques including ventilation shafts reaching to the Earth's surface (55 meters) for fresh air. It has been suggested the city was build in such a way to prevent attacks from both the ground and air above.

Suppose Derinkuyu is much older, only once adopted by the Phrygians, and truly acted as an effective means to prevent airborne attacks on our great ancient ancestors living in an earlier period when very large birds roamed the skies above.

Paleontology distinctly tells us dinosaurs went extinct 65 million years ago before the evolution of man took place from mammals of the period based on fossil findings, so perhaps pterodactyls aren't the culprit. Teratornis Woodburnensis? Teratorns had wingspans average up to 12. 5 ft across and date to the late Pleistocene, between 10,000 to 12,000 years ago, and evidence suggests they were predators, which is more reason to live underground if these giants roamed above looking for easy meals.

Living underground as a practical means for survival does make sense in a time when aerial threats were commonplace, and if this consideration was explored further, it may help archaeologists locate additional ancient sites preserved in the depths of Earth's underground by means of cavern systems. Hopi Indians, for example, believe their ancient ancestors (the Ant People) came up from the ground rather than descending from the heavens, which is similar to beliefs of the Atsabe, Chickasaw Indians, and several other native groups.

Aboriginals of Australia believe in totemic ancestors rising from the ground to walk and fly the Earth such as the Walbiri's brother spirits, Mamandabari, who rose from the ground to roam the Walbiri territory. Native tribes and aboriginals pride a close relationship with the planet, nature, and maintaining balance between the environment and their lives. The Earth is as alive as any human or animal living on its surface and requires the same respect given to ancestors.

Sion 1307

Certain controversial topics facing the world today revolve around secret societies and conspiracies tied to underground organizations. There is no question that hidden groups of people have isolated themselves from mainstream society for centuries in order to carry out executive decisions and achieve set goals in the universal order. A group of people meeting in private opens itself to speculation, hearsay, and presumptions when those on the outside do not have a clue as to what's going on, especially if the actions of the organization affect the day to day lives of large numbers of non-members.

Individuals held in high regard by mainstream society, and/or wield a significant amount of societal influence and power, act as magnets attracting attention to the organization. Proceedings on a daily basis may be uneventful and mundane, yet depending on the personality of the individual in question, conspiracy theorists perceive them as mischievous and conniving. Power and control manage to rest in the roots of non-member perceptions.

Secret societies often rely on forms of hierarchy, symbolism, and coded messages. In fact, they're so closely intertwined with deceptive matters in order to remain secretive that they inadvertently breed ideas of conspiracy without having to lift a finger.

The Prieuré de Sion, though, is a great example of a well known secret society who thrives on calculated information releases to the public in order to facilitate its mandate. Priory traditions date as early as 1099 CE in devotion to protecting and preserving the royal bloodline from the time of Jesus. According to inner circle members, the Priory holds information regarding evidence contradicting the Vatican's widely publicized belief of the resurrection of Christ and the story of his crucifixion.

The body of evidence claims to be more valuable than gold and silver including undeniable proof by certain types of artifacts. As far the the Priory is concerned, Jesus and Mary Magdalene were married. During the time of the crucifixion Mary fled with child into hiding in France to preserve the divine bloodline. Parchments now in the Vatican's possession are said to prove the Priory's stance on the subject. In fact, it's believed certain members of the Vatican are also members of the inner circle of Prieuré de Sion. They're well aware of hidden truths in Christian history but are unable to go public with the information due to complications in the positions held with the Vatican.

A majority of research about the Priory starts with Bérenger Saunière, a priest from Rennes-le-Château in France. The story explains that in 1891 Saunière discovered several parchments stashed inside the pillar of an aging church during renovations which eventually brought him to an unimaginable amount of wealth and knowledge. Villagers in Rennes-le-Château at the time testified to Saunière's sudden increase in material possessions and could not believe how a priest became so wealthy over night. There are quite a few mixed stories from the villagers as well as theorists reflecting upon the incident.

Some even believe Bérenger sold off the parchments to save his church although he did give many of the families rare gifts. Inside the church is a secret door leading to an area resembling a catacomb with an additional sealed doorway preventing further access. Several people are eager to excavate the passageway and under the church, including the mayor of Rennes-le-Château, except the French government continues to delay or block any such permit from being granted.

Despite a large number of conspiracies related to a royal bloodline, and finding the theoretical treasure of Saunière, the fact remains that Saunière was the real priest of Rennes-le-Château who did in fact run into severe money troubles and then suddenly became wealthy over night. Perhaps an old Christian treasure was discovered but instead turned over directly to the Vatican who in turn funded renovations for the church.

Templar Order sought to protect the Catholic Church by any means necessary including crusades, building defense outposts, and safe guarding the wealth of the church throughout Europe. Originally known as the Poor Fellow Soldiers of Christ and the Temple of Solomon, the Knights Templar effectively altered the course of history in their involvement with the Church. Quite a few conspiracy theories point to the Knights Templar as keepers of sacred relics and knowledge from the time of Christ. Some theories even suggest the Order is responsible for hiding the Holy Grail and Ark of the Covenant away from public prying eyes throughout the ages.

Although they are known for involvement in the crusades, many Templar were not warriors on the front-line of battle. During the rise of Templar Knights, a large amount of wealth, land,

and political power was acquired by their activities. New members were required to become poor by donating any assets, and the first concept of banking (Usury) was put into practice by the Knights Templar. Banking eventually brought about the demise of Knights Templar. France's King Philip IV tried the Order for heresy, because they refused to loan him more money, having 60 members and Grand Master Jaques de Molay arrested on Friday, October 13th in 1307. In fact, some of today's superstitions about Friday the 13th evolved from this very dark day of bad luck. Pope Clement V followed suit with King Philip and ordered the arrest of thousands of Templar Knights for heresy. According to some theories, those who survived persecution went into hiding eventually to continue traditions of protecting secrets to present day.

Unfortunately we do not have historical evidence corroborating the accounts of Jesus and the Romans despite the fact at least a dozen prominent historians were record-keeping during the time. The lack of this evidence is concerning to scholars who attempt to study the man said to perform amazing miracles. Perhaps the Templar Order managed to prevent an early age media frenzy by restricting publication as part of protecting the church. Or maybe, the Templar were protecting something much larger than the church was capable of handling, the weight of the universe.

Unidentified Creatures

All around the world we find countless eye-witness accounts and remnant evidence suggesting unknown creatures roam in the wilderness. From giant human-like mammals to giant flying birds and monstrous sea animals, the unexplored regions of the Earth invite curiosities of man to find a lost or secluded species to once in for all answer unexplained encounters with unknown creatures.

Many eye-witness encounters allude to prehistoric creatures believed to have disappeared off the face of the Earth along with dinosaurs during the last mass global extinction event. The problem with assuming these creatures died out can be found by examining known animals roaming the planet today. Crocodiles, birds, certain mammals and plants are great examples of life that survived the mass extinction and continues to thrive today.

These modern animals tend to be much smaller versions of their distant historical relatives which science attributes to changing environmental conditions over the years, narrowing their territorial size requirements for survival. Numerous overwhelming strange sightings throughout the years of animals thought to exist such as Big Foot, Nessie, and Mothman highly suggest such animals may really exist due to consistencies in sighting reports and trace evidence discovered in or around the sighting areas.

Related photographs and video footage continues to be highly scrutinized material with advancements in technology making it much easier to hoax imagery than in the past. Compelling eye-witness accounts backed with footage proven not to be a hoax by multiple professional scientific explanations tells us unknown creatures could possibly exist without our knowledge.

One of the most famous examples of compelling evidence of such animals existing is found in the 1967 Roger Patterson film shot outside of Orleans California. Even-though many scientists claim it to be a hoax, that the subject is nothing more than a man in an ape suit, many people still believe Patterson's film is authentic and point to the animal's kinetics as proof it could not be a man in a suit.

Patterson's film, along with several modern encounters caught on tape, identify a creature similar to humans with distinct qualities found consistently in sighting reports such as large feet, strong odor, fully covered in hair, and ear-piercing calls heard miles away. There are suggestions of what type of animal the Big Foot could be, such as a lost branch of human evolution hiding in the backwoods around the world or more modern humans who defected from society hundreds of years ago to live in the wilderness.

Trace remains such as fibers, hair samples, foot prints, and markings on plant life often aren't sufficient evidence to satisfy skeptics especially considering the lack of a biological body, live or dead. Hair discovered in recent years sheds a promising light for believers that unidentified creatures of some type do exist as the samples cannot be matched in the known DNA database. Attempting to identify strange whooping scream calls late at night in known sighting areas yields similar results as these very distinct noises cannot be matched up with any known animals either.

Even more compelling are reports of encounters around the world describing a very similar creature sharing many of the same characteristics. These public reports have carried on for at least the last two hundred years which meshes very well with the boom in exploration of back-country along with increased communication methods. On top of this, stories of large humanoid creatures roaming the wilderness are commonplace in the lore of native cultures all around the world. An accepted belief carried on from generation to generation hinting that we may not be alone on planet Earth, and they might not be alien at all.

An interesting correlation between reports of unknown creatures roaming the wilderness on Earth and reports of alien visitors from space. In both cases the majority of evidence stems from compelling eye-witness accounts including testimony from creditable individuals with respectable careers. Granted, a fair share of reports do encourage skepticism by the way stories are conveyed, especially when those accounts come from individuals who may be a little more eccentric than society's accepted norm. Another aspect fueling skepticism is just how profound the impact would be to Earth if either scenario proved to be true – *This makes it more difficult to believe by some.* No matter how much trace remnant evidence turns up, there are still many people who need to see a real, physical body, which makes it very difficult for witnesses who's lives have been forever changed by these encounters to be all the more convincing.

Both situations are not products of the modern world, sightings of large unknown animals and beings from space have been a close part of human history for at least thousands of years if not longer. There might be true psychological reasons why humans continue to witness the unexplained and unbelievable, or the creatures may really exist and humans are ostracizing each other because actual bodies haven't been discovered. It makes perfect sense for either such creature to be completely elusive and remain mostly undetected for thousands of years as a means of survival – *Absence can be protection and an upper hand.* The number of sightings are increasing over recent years which could be due to readily available technology in the palms of people's hands as well as an increase in human population expanding into the back-country to build homes.

Understanding why both Earth creatures and alien visitor global phenomena happens on a frequent basis can be a complex problem to tackle with many variables to take into consideration. There are psychological concepts which ironically can't be proved, in a sense, because people aren't capable of directly hearing another person's thoughts as their own; Some individuals could even be deflecting their true feelings or intentionally leaving out critical details about the experience they feel might be inconsequential.

Interviewing a number of people on both alien unexplained creature encounters as the collective subject previously described brought about some interesting results. Firstly, the majority interviewed weren't too sure about creditability of eye-witness reports, understanding those reports could be skewed at various levels, but they did find some stories very compelling and influential to their perception of the larger picture. Secondly, those interviewed want discovery to happen, to shake the world up a little. Part of the global dilemma is that humans are on top of the world, on the top of the food chain, and believe to be untouchable as kings of the hill.

Unknown creatures or extraterrestrials are a threat to mankind's position on Earth as they might be harmful to the success of the human species and it's bound to cause a stir if anything jeopardizes or is potentially devastating to mankind's position on the planet. Humans are so intelligent but they sometimes forget they're animal first, like other biological life, primitive instincts reign above all. The desire for evidence also helps prevent self-destruct.

In the bigger picture it's not a question whether or not eye-witness reports are true, it's the question of whether or not we're prepared to deal with such a situation. Until such an event happens, there will always be difficulty in attempting to figure out an effective means of communicating with unknown entities from space – *To choose between peace or war*. Perhaps civil disputes amongst ourselves throughout the ages have been indirectly preparing us for potential out-of-this-world hostile threats despite the massive destruction and life loss they've caused.

Global contingency plans are currently in place at government level to help curb the long-shot impact of an alien apocalypse but they do not account for the severe mass hysteria that would result firsthand. If a visitation happened and turned into a violent event, it is likely a large majority of the world's population would destroy themselves for survival before the foreign attack really gets into gear. By then it becomes a numbers game, and with a crippled population due to initial hysteria, humanity may end up teetering on the brink of extinction a little too close for comfort.

There are three choices we can make about this sort of situation before it happens, do nothing, hope they come in peace, or act now. Eliminating war against each other and uniting the world in peace to share in a common goal of survival in space will prepare us for anything. The effort will create a larger and stronger global defensive with the capability not only to protect our planet but also to travel the universe in the future.

Legendary Cryptids

Ancient cultures are at times most memorable by mythological stories of legendary monsters and ratifying concepts of half-man, half-beast creatures. Legendary cryptids are considered by many to primarily serve the purpose of story-telling, indicating society's willingness to sensationalize events to convey a specific message, perhaps one riddled with ulterior motives.

A peculiarity here is the fact that 99.9% of imagined concepts must be seeded, according to psychology, in order to become manifested in story-form. This highly suggests any mythological story, any imagined concept, or any tall tale fabled frenzy, must have originated from some sort of root inspiration. The trouble is really in determining exactly which parts of ancient stories aren't fabricated truths, perhaps intentionally stretched for theatrical entertainment.

Examining modern movies and storytelling might give us a little attestation as to why certain structural elements are used to relay plots. A boom in computer technology generously helped facilitate public demand for more realistic movies and provided significant improvements to live entertainment venues. If the general public strives now for a strong sense of realism in fictional storytelling, maybe it's not too far off to expect it many hundreds of years ago, as stage entertainment relied heavily on captivating audiences to similar extent.

There are countless reasons why lore, legend, and myth can become imprinted in society, but usually the message must be of great importance if the legend is to survive the ages. Even though lore is subjected to a thousand year old telephone game with stretching fish, core beliefs are often based on factual events in some way, shape, or form.

This doesn't necessarily mean a deranged jungle monkey is attacking people by throwing rocks so fast they cannot be seen, according to a hypothetical legend. It means, embellished parts of stories might sometimes be added for emphasis on the importance of danger if traveling to the area. What that danger is in the modern world, may not be known, but it could be someone protecting a gold claim with a gun in the middle of the jungle who doesn't take kindly to strangers attempting to steal his spoils. If this deranged monkey-man was instead located at the local grocery store, maybe the drawing on the refrigerator turns into a depiction of a gruesome figure with a message to keep away.

Explaining danger isn't always enough and it's far more effective to etch warnings into the mind visually. Just as mankind adapts to surviving in an unforgiving world, we have also become masters of discovery trying to explain the unknown. Those working to uncover the truth are putting man's future before themselves, to be the ones who solve some of the most perplexing problems. Cryptozoologists, for example, specifically study world inhabitants attempting to identify animals believed to exist but can't be proven to science, even past animals once deemed extinct.

It's a step off mainstream tactics to entertain ideas if such creatures do exist, just imagine the implications of needing to rewrite history books over a discovery that hid right under science's nose for thousands of years. When hundreds or even thousands of people witness seeing an unknown type of creature that science shows no record of, there must be a likely explanation to those sightings.

Technology is largely responsible for increased documentation on encounters with photography and video footage. Recent statistics claim at least 6 billion people worldwide have a mobile phone, and nearly half of those phones have a built-in camera, making it easier to photograph events as they happen. Next generation phones are becoming standardized with video capability along with Internet access and instant one-touch publishing applications.

Along with new technology comes the ability to manipulate photos and video into hoax material which ultimately hurts those legitimately searching for the truth. Skeptics have even come forward over the years admitting to fabricating evidence themselves in attempt to prove claims regarding related subject matter are false and staged by nothing more than attention seekers.

Creditable eyewitness testimony negates a good portion of hoax claims often by overwhelming margins through specific details and personal backgrounds corroborated by multiple accounts. Individual with sincere reports usually demonstrate indirectly to have no ulterior motive, no monetary or social gain, and sometimes are very much unwilling to disclose what they know publicly.

In a few prominent examples, individuals holding positions of authority are even sworn not to disclose information to anyone. This non-disclosure cycle only helps to fuel conspiracy theories and gives witnesses further reason not to release testimony. As time progresses, witnesses in these peculiar situations sometimes divulge information regardless of oath restriction and are quick to go public once the restrictive silence period is over.

Legendary Cryptids examines several strange, unexplained phenomena, some which became popularized in the 20th and 21st centuries due to technological advancements, and some of the lesser known. These creatures are theorized to exist yet lack sufficient physical evidence for science to deem as fact. Compelling eyewitness accounts help drive beliefs and sincere first-hand encounters reinforce the notion that many unknown creatures still roam the planet.

Ocean systems worldwide are a great example of areas teeming with undiscovered life due to their vastness and a significant pressure barrier hindering exploration. Land surface area of Earth is roughly 57.3 million square miles averaging to around 122 people per square mile, however, the majority of human population is concentrated around coastal areas, rivers and lakes.

Nearly 68% of world population is lives within 250 miles of a coast, leaving plenty of habitable room for unknown creatures to thrive. As density increases, more and more people are migrating into forests and mountains for places to call home. This has an adverse environmental effect especially to species who depend on the forest canopies for cover, and it begins to flush animal populations, forcing them to adapt to new environments or perish.

Combining a quickly growing human population with need for space, advances in technology, and increased interest in outdoor recreation may indicate why legitimate sightings are on the rise over the past two centuries. Perhaps the hiding locations these animals frequent are no longer sufficient for survival due to increased human activity - Essentially forcing migration to more barren terrains, or even underground into deep cavern systems. Field biologists know this sort of behavior is happening currently with known species as encounters with wild animals are on the rise as more humans move into animal territories.

Humanity

It's an honor to have energetic creatures of such astounding significance as part of the enormous collective of life on Earth coexisting with mankind. The presence of unexplained beings here in spirit, even if mainstream science may not have evidence of their existence, is indeed a privilege to witness. Cryptids are sometimes referred as conjured creatures and manifestations of imagination, sometimes from unknown regions of the mind.

However, legends of mankind demonstrate a deeper, unparalleled connectivity with life beyond simplistic psychologies of creating stories. Human life swirled into existence on Earth of all places in the universe and, along with it came the fantastic notion of consciousness. In principal, all life on this planet with or without proven consciousness, shares a root commonality in the fact life is specifically here, at this point in the universe; A presumably rare inhabitable paradise teaming with fresh oxygen, liquid water, and abundant food resources. – As far as we know Earth is life's tropical paradise of the known universe, not only because of multifariousness examples of how life can exist, but also because the multiplicity exists in a most ideal location.

Fortunately for mankind, planet Earth rests in a region of the solar system where the temperature is not too hot and not too cold, allowing life to flourish for millions of years. Science deems this near perfect area, a Goldie Locks zone, and has begun actively searching to find similar zones throughout the cosmos. It's very intriguing to think of all places in the entire universe, life is here along with imagination and creativity.

On top of what some might consider a chance location, humanity is also fortunate enough to be located in this pristine habitable zone partially protected by Jupiter, a large gaseous shield planet known for taking the brunt of asteroids bound toward Earth. These two very important features of our solar system have ensured our existence in the universe since the dawn of our creation. The sun burns just bright enough to keep us warm, and the moon moves just enough to keep the oceans mixing. Life could not be reality as we know it without these conditions, further justifying we are not simply here by coincidence, and that resulting consciousness is indeed a gift.

Until life is found elsewhere in the Universe, we must accept the fact that life is only known to be associated with Earth. This we can confirm beyond any shadow of a doubt, but it also doesn't mean life can't be found outside of our planet. Many people question whether or not life exists anywhere else in the cosmos, a definitely profound curiosity of the human condition. Are we really alone on this planet? Since we know life exists on Earth maybe because we're privileged to be located in a habitable zone, that we have our very own cosmic shields with the sun to warm us up; Yet living on Earth's surface sometimes is perceived as a much more hostile place to be. Life is not an easy existence by any means.

Over millions of years humans steadily climbed to the top of a global food chain by perseverance, ingenuity, hard work, and a little luck. The road to where mankind stands currently was very rough, even when genetic evolutionary traits pushed in our favor. At one point, ancient man learned it's easier and more efficient for survival to hunt in packs, perhaps as they once seen animals do.

Then later on, primitive man realizes it's hundreds of times more effective to use hunting strategies such as herding animals off cliffs. For the good of mankind humanity learned of extinction and detrimental loss of creatures vital to the global food chain. We learned so much in fact that domestication of livestock and preservation of foods became controlled efforts to sustain large populations over long periods of time. Throughout preservation efforts we discovered a wealth of invaluable information capable of redefining human survival as a whole, resulting in conscientious concerns of over-population, resource issues, and environmental impact facing the planet.

Nature always finds a way to balance itself over time even when results are not favorable to life on the planet. It found a way to wipe larger predatory animals off the face of Earth millions of years ago with the impact of an asteroid. Science tells us a rock fell from heavens to create a global catastrophe, eliminating entire food chains while shifting species hierarchy in the process. Perhaps there is a lesson here beyond the fact that seemingly random space rocks can destroy life on Earth.

No predator remains at the top of the food chain for long before balance of nature catches up. Even gigantic stars supernova as they consume energy at reckless rates, compared to our own sun, until all of the energy food source has been depleted. Naturally humans are concerned with the threat of space debris destroying everything as we know it. This means an asteroid hitting the Earth, although inherently random, could be considered a type of predator to mankind in a sense, because it jeopardizes our survival. Locating, predicting, and dealing with Earth impacts is a very important emerging science and well justified. Perhaps asteroids act as one of many ways of balancing life in the universe, presuming life exists elsewhere, when worlds become incapable of sustaining an over-efficient top predator.

As humans we know asteroids are not the only detrimental events threatening mankind's survival. Disease sweeps the planet on regular intervals inadvertently culling parts of the human population. Science has managed to eradicate many microscopic menaces but still needs to stand on the front line against new strains and mutations. Simply, it's near impossible at this moment in technology to completely rid the world of life threatening diseases and it may not become a reality as we continue to explore distant reaches of the universe.

Discovering new life also warrants the possibility of discovering new diseases. Nature might sometimes attempt to restore balance by introducing variations of diseases capable of abolishing an entire planet of life, and by chance, previously unknown diseases may have hitched a ride with comets and meteors, surviving the rigors of space only to wreak havoc on Earth. Modern theories do suggest life on Earth is the result of water and organisms seeding the planet; Malicious organisms arriving in the same manor isn't too far off.

Maybe there's truly a factor of randomness as with asteroid impacts, that nature once tugged on a giant theoretical slot machine of creation resulting in a dial of cherry, cherry, orange. Thus, life of a specific type shall appear in the cherry, cherry, orange quadrant of the universe as predefined by a whole slew of other unorthodox methods.

In this hypothetical, nature counts how many fractional skips a molecule of helium makes across a partially solidified lava lake measured down to the 4,022nd decimal place. Whatever that outcome is shall be applied as a constant to the slot machine of creation's results, and may change for the next subset of life to follow as a completely different catalyst is decided. For some reason life exists here of all places in the universe and however that might be determined remains unknown.

This is our existence and the biggest theoretical question of anyone's lifetime seems to ask, why? Why did the giant slot machine select cherry, cherry, orange instead of cherry, lime, apple when deciding where life is to be placed? Did it also spin cherry, cherry, kiwi calling into existence creatures very similar to human, placing them on the same planet for us to one day discover each other? We have intrinsic reasons to truly understand ourselves for pushing forward everyday, it's a way of finding value in our reality, but we also exist for reasons we are not capable of understanding or explaining, much like the legends we create and continue to keep alive. Stories of our past are part of us on a deeper level, a way to teach, learn, and remember what made us who we are today.

During the stone age especially, describing the world to others became necessary to ensure success. Knowing where and where not to go could mean the difference between living and dying - Our ancestors must have excelled at this in order for us to be here today, and their hard work still applies in the modern world as people seek to explore some of the more remote regions of Earth. Local knowledge of the land and its animals is crucial to avert potentially unknown consequences. In order to accurately reference parts of the world to others, mankind developed a communication system unlike anything else in the known animal kingdom.

Pictogram language on cave walls could teach offspring about encounters before getting into them. Planned hunts with multiple people could be strategical for everyone at once like calling plays on a football field. This huge step brought forth greater efficiency, less deaths, and more downtime to explore. It stimulated development of the imagination and a craving to figure out the world around us, eventually incorporating great detail of the outside world.

Before spoken language, how would one describe large bats to others aside from hand gestures? Drawing the bat on a cave wall gives additional detail even if a stone carving may skew the actual shape and form. Perhaps the body reminded people at the time of a tiny human with large wings and became replicated as such on a cave wall. Maybe the bat was tormenting people and one person stood up, killed it, and became a hero portrayed as conqueror of bats. Great men who perform great feats are forever part of the piles of society. However the heroic story is told, the underlying message remains the same with intent to bolster an individual's contributions to the world as a whole.

J.C. Vintner

Monsters of the Deep

Harmonious with man stepping aboard floating vessels to traverse the bountiful oceans of the world are legends of colossal sea monsters such as the Kraken and Colossal squid, capable of destroying even the largest of ships and devouring the crew. The deep dark blue waters separating land masses of the world have captivated man since the dawn of time as they sustain life both in the sea and on land, but can be quick to take it away. To our knowledge like the heavens above, giant bodies of water seemed impassible to the depths for many thousands of years.

Even in the modern age, the task remains very dangerous and difficult, making Earth's oceans the largest unexplored portion of our planet by far. No wonder our ancient ancestors may have developed fears or felt intimidated by the deep blue, after all it was anyone's guess what lurked below on the way to a horizon which seemed to suddenly drop off into nowhere from a distance. Present day Oceanographers have put some sea fears to rest even-though a very tiny portion of what's known to exist has been uncovered. A single submersible visit to hydrothermal vents and underwater mud volcanoes in the Marianas Trench commonly finds many new, previously unidentified species. Life found here is capable of withstanding temperatures up to 300 degrees Celsius while being subjected to over eight tons per square inch of pressure. To discover life flourishing in the most hostile, extreme environments on Earth is encouraging to several disciplines of science, including those searching for life on other planets throughout the cosmos.

Robust life fills oceans of the world in many shapes and forms sometimes even considered alien-like by appearance alone. Taxonomy suggests 8.7 million species of life cover the entire planet and at least half of those species make their home in the sea. Recent estimates claim at least a million species have not been found or identified according the Census of Marine Life. Discovering cryptids in the oceans might be much more likely due to these numbers, there are simply more places for these legendary creatures to hide and remain undetected. In fact, that is exactly what the fabled colossal squid is believed to do. For ages colossal squid were believed to exist but never proven aside from encounters near the ocean's surface and partially decayed biological matter found washed up on the world's beaches.

Many stories over the years detailed events with giant squid including mentions by Aristotle, but only myths and legends dared to mention something even bigger, the colossal. A discovery in

1925 uncovered two colossal tentacles found in a sperm whale stomach, linking the two animals together while providing initial proof these massive creatures do exist. In 2007 legends turned to reality as a New Zealand fishing vessel captured the largest known intact cephalopod in recorded history, weighing around 990 lbs. while measuring 33 foot long. Characteristics of colossal squid are nearly identical to giant squid except they have a wider and shorter body with tentacles featuring swiveling hooks theorized to be responsible for scar marks commonly found on sperm whales. The whales have long been known to feast on octopus and squid from partially digested remnants found in carcasses.

Dissections have also found squid beaks larger than the monster netted in 2007, highly suggesting much larger colossal squid exist. In July 2012 a broadcasting company called NHK and the Discovery Channel successfully filmed a giant squid for the first time in history estimated to be around 23 foot long diving just south of Tokyo. According to the Smithsonian the longest giant squid on record measures 43 feet despite rumored lengths, but this does provide interesting clues to the idea of a Kraken or similar type of giant sea monster.

Cephalopod species reach maturity quickly and face a shorter life expectancy, meaning that even if super massive squid or octopus exists, the window for discovering it before death is quite narrow, thus playing a significant role in how elusive these creatures are. Many encounters with giant squid, colossal squid, and even giant octopus have occurred not far from coastlines around the world as they possibly rise to the surface for feeding. Given the monstrosity of giant squid and the possibility of even larger colossal squid, it seems like a perfect fit to Norwegian myths of a Kraken capable of snapping the largest ships in two.

Suppose that every once in a while one of these colossal monsters grows abnormally large, either due to environmental influence or rare hormone conditions, and then rises to the surface to feed perhaps on the same prey caught by a fishing vessel that just happened to be in the area. The fishermen unknowingly nab a colossal with tentacles long enough to wrap around the boat as they pull it out of the water. Indeed this would be a frightening experience and definitely something to remember especially if it happened at night, but it doesn't seem totally out of the question for such an event to happen in rare occurrence.

A fishing vessel scenario lends feasibility to this sort of freak event yet it can't quite explain Kraken attacks on merchant ships in the same light. Given a potential size of giant or colossal squid or octopus compared to the size of ships at the time, it's not out of the question to think the

Kraken would've been as real as day and a true threat to sailors. Clearly these types of creatures do exist but perhaps the embellished portions of their stories reside in the monster's intentions. Often they're portrayed as gigantic ravenous animals who seek out ships traversing high seas without an inkling to the fact encounters may have been unintentionally provoked in competition for prey. Or maybe there is a completely different type of creature out there lurking the depths of the world's oceans.

Giant or colossal cephalopods have commonalities with their smaller, more common cousins, such as an ability to hunt using bioluminescence; Similar to shining a flashlight at the surface of a lake or to attract fish at night when recreational fishing. The idea of bioluminescence in massive creatures may partially explain some sightings of USO's or Unidentified Submersible Objects. When a giant squid rises to the surface at night for feeding, using bioluminescence, it's quite possible eyewitnesses might mistake it for something otherworldly.

An onlooker may only see the glowing light and a faint outline of the figure creating it, not being able to make heads or tails out of what they were looking at. Squid generally feed at night, sometimes running along the surface a few meters down, and might be attracted to lights on the boat or certain frequencies of sound emitting from the engine. It also explains why fishing sonar might pickup very large pings as described in some USO reports. However, the only known squid to actually breach the surface and fly as USO encounters claim unidentified ships do, is the Japanese Flying Squid, which is much too small to match up with most USO reports. Although there are plenty of USO sightings to form plausible explanation(s), the hard evidence science requires is often lacking to help corroborate eyewitness stories.

On the controversy, sometimes plenty of tangible samples aren't even enough for positive identification. Strange biological masses found around the world wash up on ocean shorelines regularly with a significant portion of the incidents remaining unidentifiable. These blobs of organic goo, Globsters as they've been titled, can be a disturbing sight and seem to fit science fiction more than any sort of real life scenario; Fortunately for most encounters the blob is not alive and is not trying to gorge on everything in its path. Globsters are difficult to identify at first because they appear as a mess of organic matter somewhat resembling a creature.

Biological matter decomposes differently in water, especially in cooler temperatures that inhibit bacterial action and enzyme decay. In fact, wooden ship wrecks are so well preserved under water for long periods of time due to a similar process, and attempting to raise them risks accelerated decay. As organic matter finds itself under less pressure it may expand to match the new volume. While being exposed directly to oxygen the bacterial action and enzyme decay can resume. If an animal carcass exhibited the same type of pressure change as ship parts on the ocean floor rising to the surface, bloating may be slightly irregular and then exacerbated once decomposition is thrown back into its regular state. Scientists are able to identify what creature(s) makeup the majority of mass but many positive identifications of Globsters require DNA matching to be certain. Often these messy globs tend to be remains of decomposing whales or sharks, and some are speculated to be carcasses of decaying cephalopods.

Another suggested theory claims the masses to be organic remnants collecting together by ocean currents, fusing together with pressure over time, and then washing onto beaches where they're usually discovered. Globsters are an odd phenomena even when they can be properly explained. Large ocean animal remains are often scavenged at sea, either near the surface as they sink or on the sea floor, well before they have a chance to wash up on shore.

Decaying carcasses provide a vital food resource for many creatures and help create a feature of the ocean known as Marine Snow, whereby bits organic matter slowly settle to the sea bed in concentrations dense enough to appear like snow falling from the sky. Research into the subject is currently unclear as to whether or not Globsters find the world's beaches after being rejected by scavengers due to a chemical signature, by some sort of disease, or by a sequence of normal events that instead pushes the body to a shoreline instead of toward the sea bed.

J.C. Vintner

Amphibious Humans

Combining features of aquatic animals with humans has long been a part of folklore and mainstream science fiction, with the motif appearing in several movie productions where strange serpent-like creatures seem to enjoy tormenting humans. To Ufologists, humanoid reptiles are a race of aliens responsible for countless abductions, and to conspiracy theorist David Icke, Reptilians have the ability to shape-shift and drink blood.

According to Icke, these reptile people arrived on Earth from the Alpha Draconis (Dragon) star system, located around 303 light years away, bound and bent to take over the world by possessing or replacing influential people in higher positions of power. Although David's conspiracies and science fiction stories might seem a little beyond scientific explanation, the idea of lizard or aquatic-like humanoids has long been a part of human history. For example, the previously isolated Dogon Tribe in West Africa believes in deities called Nommos, an amphibious race visiting the Earth on a sky ship from Sirius. They're not the only ones.

Amphibious and reptile humanoid deities are referenced in several ancient cultures such as Greek, Chinese, Egyptian, Aztec, Zoroastrian, Portuguese, Hindu and Islamic. There is certainly something curious about human desires to depict themselves as part snake, reptile, or any other animal for that matter. Perhaps these accounts are indications ancient deities did exist in the flesh, spawning legends for future generations based on real events. Or maybe it's a way of emphasizing extraordinary abilities of presumed deities to show what the gods are capable of as intimidation to humans. There is also an idea these sorts of amalgamations are simply imaginative beliefs and manifested curiosities of what a human would be like if actually blessed in part with specific characteristics of an animal. Some theorists even suggest this type of hybridization is evidence our ancient ancestors (and/or gods) experimented with transplant surgeries and DNA in order to create them.

Modern sightings of lizard-like humanoids continue to happen although they're not quite as common as reports of other creatures like Bigfoot, and they're often taken far less seriously due to both the type of controversies and countless hoaxes. In 1955, a businessman called the police after witnessing four humanoids with faces like frogs, crouching under a bridge not far from Loveland, Ohio. In 1972, police transcripts were apparently leaked to media and falsely reported by embellishing details of the creatures spotted.

The officer was interviewed and a new story soon emerged claiming the businessman did not see a monster, and that the animals were likely someone's escaped pets. Spun out of control by the media, the officer claimed, recounting previous testimony. Given the time frame of this reported encounter, it's quite possible there might have been outside factors which caused news media or the businessman to react as they did. Sequels to the recent 1954 Godzilla release were showing in theaters around this time, along with a booming Sci-Fi following, suggesting a possible seed influence.

Movies of the era sparked the imaginations of many, perhaps just enough that some people might believe these monsters are lurking in unknown shadowy areas of real life. Unfortunately, a single documented case by public officials isn't really sufficient claim to believe people genuinely were seeing lizard humanoids in Ohio. The media may have truly tried to draw attention to themselves over a benign event, or it could be simply a case of new entertainment affecting the general public.

A similar hysteria happened in 1938 on a much larger scale when Orson Welles presented

War of the Worlds as a series of radio broadcasts. His news bulletin style show presented enough details to cause a few people to actually believe Earth was being invaded by aliens at those very moments. Orson's broadcast was a lesson well learned. Along with World War II stress, it caused panic that may have been exemplified as newspapers seemed to feel threatened by a new age radio medium. Whether or not the general public realized War of the Worlds was fictional, it was told in such a way to create a large scale public reaction. From this it's suffice to say that entertainment media is capable of influencing what people believe, and in some cases enough to alter their public behaviors.

This might even be a contributing factor to explaining how at least thirteen witnesses in 1988 claimed they observed a lizard humanoid creature in South Carolina, around Browntown Road in Lee County. Christopher Davis first reported an encounter with the creature which lead to other eyewitnesses stepping forward with closely related stories.

A few years earlier, in 1982, Wes Craven's Swamp Thing was released in theaters; Entirely filmed in Charleston South Carolina 128 miles south of, yes - Lee County. The sequel, Return of Swamp Thing, was filmed to the west in Savannah Georgia and released in 1989, one year after sightings were officially reported. Is it possible that movie cast and crew were trekking through the swamps for footage and went off-course at some point, perhaps passing by not far from Browntown Road, a two hour drive from Charleston? Could it be that as other witnesses waited to come forward, Christopher did the same, after they accidentally stumbled upon filming for either one of the Swamp Thing movies toward the south and west?

We know it's easy to get turned around in lush areas of thick swamp lands; Over time trees and waterways can become disorientating and begin to look similar in every direction. Imagine trying to film it or follow acting scripts of a movie during the trek. Maybe the Lizard Man of South Carolina is a case of mistaken identity in this sense, or one intentionally influenced by entertainment media in a more obfuscated fashion. A failed publicity stunt in attempt to generate hype if indeed the sightings around Browntown were an attempt to stir public controversy. Instead they became local legend even after Christopher became nationally famous, hardly impacting the box office. The Lizard-man might really be a true cryptid, and just a mere coincidence that Swamp Thing movies were filmed in the same area. However, without any eyewitness reports in the past 24 years since the second release of the movie, it seems highly unlikely.

Legends of amphibious reptile monster encounters are traditionally entwined with swamps in North America, but then become seafaring as tales of hybrid human-fish creatures and strange sea anomalies are abundant with ship and sailing crews. Mermaids, Mermen, Sea monks, Siren, and Nymphs have all played significant roles in sea lore, sometimes saving ships from danger and at other times luring crews to their demise. One series of mermen stories provides insight into the perception of our ancient relatives when an animal living off the coast of Denmark is described to be a cross between a Fryer Monk and a fish. Sea Monks were depicted in the Book of Days as this literal representation and later became known as the giant squid thanks to the efforts of zoologist Japetus Steenstrup.

Other researchers believe these strange creatures found off Denmark were just misinterpreted sightings of walrus, sharks, or seals, although close examination of the drawings reveals the shape and characteristics of a giant squid to be more likely. To Cryptozoologists, there isn't always sufficient evidence to explain odd stories and legends from the past especially when a significant amount of time has lapsed.

The Sea Monk case clearly shows an example of how a few of our ancestors interpreted creatures never seen before. Instead of seeing these animals as a completely separate species of biological life, they instead focused on observed human-like qualities. Key features of 'curious fish' (giant squid) like the large eyes, tentacles, and head shape stood out from the distance enough to propose a theory; Be it one based on spiritual influence, along with enough detail for science to eventually come to a plausible and likely conclusion.

Lake Monsters

Of all the cryptids believed to exist around the world, Nessie is one of the most sensationalized by media coverage and speculation. Many people know the story of Ness and have entertained themselves with the concept of an supposedly extinct dinosaur swimming in the depths of a Scottish lake. Controversial photographs and eyewitness accounts helped Loch Ness gain attention while portraying an astounding question asking whether or not dinosaurs could still exist.

The Surgeon's photo, in particular, depicts a shadowy figure estimated to be located around 4 km from the camera. Incredibly, this figure strangely resembles a type of plesiosaur considered only to be part of fossil record. Multiple theories have attempted to debunk Nessie, ranging from a bobbing tree trunk to optical illusions and intentional hoaxes. Despite skepticism, many eyewitness testimonies have stood up to the onslaught and continue to spark the imagination of folks wondering what really might live deep below Loch Ness.

Hundreds of years ago, Scotland's Lochs were home to a Christian revolution, as Evangelist, Saint Columba traveled north toward Pictland in a mass effort to reform local belief systems. He was very successful and gained quite a popular adoration by in part to Adoman, the 9th Abbot of Iona, who documented Columba's travels in prideful detail. Adoman worked to exemplify feats of Columba by recording many miracle events, one of which some believe might indicate Columba encountered Nessie for the first time in history, late in the 6th century. Adoman's account describes Saint Columba running into men burying a body previously attacked by a water monster called Niseag.

The men took this body out of the River Ness by hook and proceeded to ask another man to row a moored cable out to the boat. While this man was swimming, a beast came after him, but then fled when Saint Columba spoke and presented the sign of the cross to it. An estimated size or further details were not provided. We do know, based on a later mention in the accounts, the water creature likely wasn't a whale of some sort. In those details, Saint Columba performs another miracle by preventing a whale from attacking men setting to sea.

There are several known legends of water dwelling monsters in Scottish, Irish and Pictish history. Saint Columba's experience may boil down to how ancient cultures in the area described animals at the time, even if those creatures seemed to only exist for mythological purposes by modern science. Two such creatures exist in Pictish folklore evident by symbols found in their ancient stone carvings. One resembles the shape of a dolphin, dragon, horse or elephant and is popularized today as the Pictish Beast. The other is the Water-horse, or highland bull, claimed to haunt pools and lochs to lure children to their deaths.

In both cases we find distinct features which could match up with Columba's encounter to suggest it might be a play on folklore for the benefit of an Evangelistic journey, but nothing quite specific enough for plausible identification of a past Nessie relative. Both Irish and Scottish lore talk of similar beasts, namely the River Wolf, Water Hound, Irish Crocodile, and Dobhar-Chu. Although these animals are traditional described as half-dog / half -fish, they eerily fit along with Columba and some Nessie descriptions.

Modern science and archaeological record might have a logical answer which unfortunately may not be a sole surviving Plesiosaur as some hoped it would be. Characteristics of Nessie sightings tend to fit Plesiosuchus, a dinosaur who disappears from fossil record roughly around 4 million years ago. Characteristics of water beast sightings such as the Dobhar-Chu tend to fit another dinosaur called Dakosaurus, a prehistoric whale alive during the same era as Plesiosuchus.

Given there is sufficient archaeological evidence to say both creatures went extinct millions of years ago, and the unlikeliness of either animal surviving undetected until a couple thousand years ago, it seems as though Nessie is not a lone dinosaur. This is science's take on it, requiring biological evidence of either dinosaur to prove otherwise, and to their credit, Loch Ness itself was formed around 10,000 years ago by a receding glacier. If Nessie is a Plesiosuchus, Plesiosaur, or related dinosaur from millions of years ago, then likely she had to move into the Loch after its creation. Life without doubt is full of strange enough phenomena.

Maybe Niseag could be one of those rare animals who survived in the deep ocean despite science claiming the improbable. The world's ocean system is vast and plenty large enough to sustain a breeding population of dinosaurs who managed to survive a catastrophic extinction event 65 million years ago. In fact, many ocean dwelling creatures may have been protected during the initial fallout long enough for food chain cycles to replenish, and it wouldn't be out of the ordinary for life to flourish through catastrophe once again.

There is perhaps yet another angle to help explain Nessie. By reconstructing certain elements of local folklore we discover characteristics of a beast which might be responsible for stimulating Nessie sightings. Starting with the name, Ness - Loosely translates to a cape, promontory, headland, fore-land, Naze (Eastern England Headland), or head. Niseag, as referred to by Saint Columba, is a Scottish Gaelic female name for Little Ness. Possibly a significant clue here - Little head.

Many eyewitness accounts and photographs describe a creature with a smaller head at the end of what could be described as a long neck. Hence a suggested identification of a plesiosaur even though we know these dinosaurs had to overcome tremendous odds to be placed in Loch Ness by the 20th century. Known species in Scottish lakes don't fit Ness descriptions very well, but what if perhaps a known species from another location moved into Scottish territory, using the lochs as safe haven due to increased human population in the previous area?

It lends merit to why more sightings have occurred in the past century than ever before. The giant otter, for example, is a large animal which fits both descriptions of Columba's water monster and modern Nessie sightings including photographic evidence. Encounters in the past couple hundred years have sometimes been attributed to common otters who are known to live in the Loch Ness area. We know average sized otters are capable of making this area their home. What about this possibility of giant otters moving in on the territory?

Firstly, populations of giant otters generally span from central to north Africa, some distance from Scottish locks, but that could be changing due to recent human impact. Giant otter are steadily at increased risk of extinction due to over-hunting for pelts and food. It's possible groups of giant otters are slowly being pushed further and further north over human activity, perhaps even finding their way through the Mediterranean coastal waters, or inland rivers over time to reach northern parts of Europe.

Life on Earth adapts for survival instinctively and it wouldn't be surprising to see a species to relocate if they're constantly undergoing significant threats to their survival. Giant otter are carnivorous and territorial, they would not hesitate to demonstrate aggressive behavior especially if confronted by humans, just as described in the Saint Columba case. Average giant otter sizes range from 4.9 to 5.6 foot long body length with a tail reaching up to another 2.4 feet.

Reports in Africa suggest males are capable of reaching a length of at least 7.9 feet, and with the tail we're looking at a pretty large creature here. Along with the size of giant otters, they also share a unique ability as their smaller cousins, periscope behavior. When a giant otter periscopes, a decent portion of their body is out of the water, giving the look of a long narrow trunk or neck. Their heads are smaller in relation, just as a Little Ness might indicate. Short, webbed feet of the otter may sometimes give a flipper-like appearance, also described in some Nessie reports. Also, there are Spanish names for giant otters that draw close resemblance to Scottish and Irish lore. The Lobo De Rio (River Wolf) and Perro De Agua (Water Dog) both fit water devils and monsters.

Even more intriguing is the giant otter fitting these descriptions as a half fish, half dog beast. Legends in Ireland speak of Doyarchu, a dog-like otter with large dark orange flippers sighted around Omey Island and Cornwall, further described on a gravestone as a tragic event happening in the 17th century. Could it be that

Niseag is really just a larger than normal giant otter, perhaps even a colossal otter, surviving at a distance from a seriously threatened diminishing population? Bernard Heuvelmans, respected father of Cryptozoology once named this type of extinct species Hyperhydra egedei, or Super Otter, claiming it spanned 60 to 100 foot in length and lived between Greenland and Norway. Maybe Bernard wasn't too far off in his presumptions if indeed Giant Otters have an undiscovered relative residing in the cooler waters toward the north.

Ideas of a giant sea monsters living in the dark depths of ancient lakes are not uncommon and stories revolving around lake dwelling giants have been around for centuries. Many times as eyewitness accounts reach scientific scrutiny, explanation usually points to floating debris, bird swarms, optical illusions, and misidentified lake life such as common otters. Each cryptid features unique details pertinent to the respective area's history which helps in attempting to positively identify what creature it might be.

In the age of computer generated realities science will continue with a hard-nosed approach until any cryptid is physically obtained and/or witnessed by scientific professionals. However, in the days long before computers and cameras, people relied on word of mouth, oral traditions, and documentations that only reached a small fraction of the masses compared to today's media outlets. Hoaxing for attention or other ulterior motives still happened centuries ago, it's always important to consider this as a possibility with any myth or legend.

Some say the Sea Monster of Cape Ann fits in this category, that early reports from the 17th century were likely identifications of a more common animal embellished to fit the tales of Massachusetts explorers. Even though skeptics are quick to dismiss Cape Ann monster accounts, they don't seem to have a retort for a similar monster appearing in Wampanoag Indian mythology as the Horned Serpent. Two Indians were along with Englishmen according to John Josselyn's report from a journey off the coast of New England, two Indians who convinced the English not to attempt killing the sea serpent they witnessed. Rightfully so, considering cultural beliefs of the Wampanoag view the Horned Serpent in association with Hobbomock, the destructive spirit of death. If it were not killed outright, Hobbomock will have his vengeance. From this we know the Cape Ann monster was not first discovered by Josselyn. Despite these problems we still sometimes discover stories from the past that are very compelling with so many unique aspects the legends slowly begin to corroborate themselves.

The Nessie of America, some might say, is in many ways similar to the mysterious creature causing a ruckus every so often in Loch Ness,

Scotland. Big Rem, or Champ, is a theorized plesiosaur residing in a deep freshwater lake running along the New York, Vermont state line called Lake Champlain. Fossil record indicates Champlain was once a salt water glacial lake, aptly named Lake Vermont, which drained very quickly by a failing ice dam around 12,000 years ago, creating a flood of Biblical proportion and turning it into a body of water known as the Champlain Sea – An inlet connected directly to the Atlantic Ocean.

It's possible Champ became trapped in the Champlain area when the ice dam broke like a minnow in a giant beach puddle, retaining habitat in the newly formed Champlain Sea even beyond the time of its recession around 10,000 years ago. Alternatively, and like Nessie, it's also possible Champ survived for millions of years in the deep ocean and found its way to Lake Champlain after it was formed well after the the ice dam broke and sea retreated.

Lake Champlain's outflow today travels by way of the Richelieu River, north to the St. Lawrence River confluence which then routes toward the Gulf of St. Lawrence and the Atlantic ocean. Access to Champlain from the ocean is still possible although travel would be hindered against the outflow of Lake Ontario and Richelieu river.

The trip also means overcoming Chambly rapids,
a dangerous section of Richelieu with shallow
areas capable of producing surf-sized waves
during annual spring melt.

Although Lake Champlain's history gives plausible explanation of how a giant sea creature or surviving dinosaur might be making the lake its home, scientists still believe the scenario is unlikely. Eyewitnesses and marine biologists are aware of the presence of large lake sturgeon in various parts of Champlain. Sturgeon are prehistoric looking with rows of protruding bone plates, and can grow up to nine feet long over a life span of roughly 100 years, making it an ideal explanation to Champy sightings. Except, Champy reports often sing to a different tune. A reptile-like monster, between 25 to 30 foot long, serpent features, head the shape of a horse, a scale-like appearance - Indicating Champ is something entirely different altogether.

Witnesses say they know exactly what sturgeon look like, claiming Champ is definitely not a sturgeon. Hundreds of reported sightings have occurred since Samuel de Champlain first charted the lake and it was his sighting in 1609 to become the first documented record to our knowledge.

Prior to Champlain's discovery, as he soon learned, the local Iroquois and Abenaki Indians already had names for this mysterious water monster, calling it Chousarou or Taoskok. In Iroquoian mythology there are references to the Horned-Serpent, a water creature both rancorous and pleasant depending on the situation, and responsible for creating storms above the lakes.

Champie is one of the more popularized sea monster legends in America and, there are others. On the western coast, not far from the Canadian border, is an inlet water system channeling the Pacific Ocean around Vancouver Island. In this waterway are many islands, a unique ecosystem, and several sightings over the last two centuries of an unknown animal referred to as Cadborosaurus willsi. Eyewitness accounts are similar to those reported in Lake Champlain and Loch Ness except for one crucial difference which stands alone.

Visual confirmations of Caddy will sometimes involve a multiple headed creature or heard of creatures. Cryptozoologists have ruled out suspected animals in the area such as moose water crossings and determined Caddy is most likely an unknown species. Prominent features of this sea monster include identifiable webbed flippers, a large fan-shaped tail (like a pipefish), and serpent characteristics. Also like Nessie and Champ, the Cadborosaurus has roots in local native legends reaffirming these sightings are not just modern phenomena.

Ancient encounters with sea monsters have occurred along the United States Pacific Coast, ranging from San Francisco all the way up to Alaska evident by recorded mythologies from the Manhousat, Sechelt and Comox Indians. Further inland, just north of the American Mexican border, the Maricopa Tribe of Arizona references Hailkotat as a sea monster who rewards bravery with its power of strength and to cure illness, transforming a young Indian into a medicine-man. As with legends further up the coast, Hailkotat lore is centralized around a sea-accessible area following the Gila and Colorado rivers, and similar to Lake Champlain, sea animals here would need to travel against the current to make the journey.

Of all the sightings up and down the coast there is one known exception where a legendary sea monster resides disconnected from any ocean body of water. Lake Okanagan is a fair distance from the Pacific Ocean, making it unlikely that an unknown creature living in the depths of the world's oceans found its way there. This lake is located in British Columbia and by local legend is home to Ogopogo (Naitaka by native tradition), theorized by Cryptozoologist Karl Shuker to be a King Lizard from the Late Eocene era.

The suggestion by Karl that Ogopogo is an animal believed to have lived approximately 35 million years ago still surviving to this day in a nearly isolated lake is a difficult theory to accept for most scientists. However, Shuker brings up interesting points by referencing Basilosaurus fossils found in Louisiana, Mississippi, Alabama, Egypt and Pakistan as evidence King Lizards were at one point in the area. Many characteristics connect eyewitness reports to fossil record, further indicating these types of creatures once lived not only in North America, but also around the world.

To point a finger at a few King Lizards surviving against long odds for 35 million years is a brave accusation, and there might need to be an even bolder explanation to contend with the lack of a strong breeding population to survive in a confined area for so long. There is also another issue which doesn't help Karl's case at all. Lake Okanagan is a glacial-formed lake, carved out by a south moving glacier, dated by sediment to only *45,000 years ago*.

If Ogopogo is indeed a King Lizard, another theory is necessary to explain how they traveled so far inland prior to the time of local river and lake creation, or perhaps it's a different animal altogether.

Presume these legendary cryptids are actually the animals they're theorized to be according to eyewitness accounts. How an ancient species of animals were able to survive for millions of years, resulting in a modern presence is a largely unknown and perceived to be highly unlikely, but that doesn't necessarily rule out the possibility of it happening. In the case of Ogopogo we know a glacier retreated to form the lake. What if perhaps a plesiosaur, or small groups of plesiosaurs in this area became trapped in the ice by an extreme weather event, one that somehow froze the animal inside the glacier?

The glacier slowly thawed over time, eventually released its victim into the new lake, successfully reintroducing a long lost species. Given this type of scenario we have a lot to contend with as far as feasibility, let alone the odds of it happening. Yet it's not quite as far fetched as one might think at first glance. Some animals are capable of entering a Cryptobiotic state whereby metabolic function stops completely, and they're able to suspend themselves in this manor for as long as it takes. Once conditions return to acceptable levels, the creature continues life as it did prior to entering Cryptobiosis.

If select species of dinosaurs were capable of this type of survival behavior, it seems much more plausible eyewitnesses have encountered true relics from ancient times living in a modern world. Would dinosaurs maintain suspended animation for millions of years though?

According to Cryptobiosis theories, it might happen provided conditions in which an animal entered this state remain consistent for the duration, otherwise the animal would enter and leave its Cryptobiotic state each time conditions fluctuate enough to trigger it. Dinosaur biology is tricky to determine considering living specimens are not available. Scientists have limited evidence to go by in determining all biological factors contributing to the full life of a dinosaur and it will take many more years of research to determine if any of Earth's larger ancient species were capable of similar hibernation or Cryptobiotic states found in plants and animals of today.

Dragonosaurs

The Bible talks in detail an enormous, fire breathing, twisted coil creature called Leviathan in the book of Job. In most ways traditionally, Leviathan fits descriptions of dragons found in ancient cultures around the world, either as a large snake of the sea, or large flying snake from the heavens. Characteristics of dragons commonly emphasize the mixture of a lizard and serpent while being portrayed as dangerously destructive and wiser than man although there are legends of friendly snakes who are inclined to help mankind. Stories of drakon (Greek) creatures date back thousands of years well beyond their modern age title. One can't help but notice the strange resemblance of flying serpent dragons, or sea dragons, to that of artistic reconstructions of ancient dinosaurs.

Many features are very similar especially in the case of wyverns, with two large clawed feet and a body shape (including the tail) similar to carnivorous dinosaurs. How would nearly every major civilization around the world make reference to a dinosaur type creature well before archaeologists pieces any of the bones together? Some theorists suggest ancient civilizations might have lived alongside dinosaurs as evident in ancient artwork such as the Ica Stones and carvings from the Aztecs. These ideas are highly contested due to an enormous gap in accepted dating methods between dinosaurs and the aforementioned cultures, but their artifacts do provide some sort of indication that our ancient ancestors may have been influenced in some way by creatures of this type. Details present in a number of sculptures are suspect of actually seeing creatures on a basis regular enough to accurately represent them in pottery, stone and clay; Features in some cases are absolutely astounding how closely the figures represent present day depictions of certain species of dinosaurs, giving the idea dinosaurs may not be as old as mainstream theories suggest.

In 2006 a Tyrannosaurus Rex discovered in Montana revealed something never before witnessed and previously thought impossible, traces of blood vessels and cellular structures. Some consider this discovery as smoking gun evidence dinosaurs did not die out entirely in one final blaze. Unfortunately ancient Rex blood and soft tissue doesn't indicate when it died as it only provides evidence blood survived for millions of years as the skeleton is dated. Perhaps the 2006 find opens a doorway to new blood preservation techniques while suggesting that if all conditions (as in the found sample) are met, blood might actually preserve indefinitely.

There is yet another issue when it comes to dinosaur bones. Generally ancient bones are believed to reveal their age by measuring uranium and potassium isotopes of rocks they're discovered in, since bones do not contain necessary elements with a long enough half-life to measure accurately. Using this method is a magnet to skeptical barrage often followed up with Carbon-14 dating, in which case the same dinosaur bones yield a much more recent date when compared to the rocks encasing them. Ineffective Carbon-14 dating methods are often referred in theories of humans and dinosaurs coexisting, but the dating in this manor can be easily contaminated with organic matter decaying in and around fossilized bones. Carbon-14 has a half-life of 5,730 years rendering it only effective on samples no older than 50,000 years, so in essence, measuring the C-14 of a dinosaur bone is great for returning the age of organic matter stuck to its surfaces.

Consulting hard evidence of 65 million year old monster animal skeletons reveals an intriguing view of native oral traditions in that it suggests alternative explanation for said legends. Theorists have proposed that perhaps our ancient relatives were alive during the same time these creatures roamed the Earth. Fossil record effectively bypasses the theory as it shows paleontologists significant lapses between human and dinosaur periods in the planet's evolutionary history, largely due to available evidence. What if there is supporting evidence out there, somewhere, to show us that our ancient ancestors indeed lived alongside prehistoric type animals? Maybe not those described by the current fossil record, but animals we have yet to discover because of where their remains might be located.

Our relatives relied heavily on oral tradition in their daily lives and they created many of the myths and legends we know today. Could it be possible that our ancestors have these stories as a result from first-hand encounters with the real deal hundreds of thousands of years ago, or is there another explanation?

Paleontologists are literally only scratching the surface of biological life history. Geologists know very well the planet's land masses shift while essentially recycling themselves over many millions of years; Making it difficult to find many of the missing links in animal evolutionary history as some of them are likely being pushed beyond current human reach. The world's deepest fossil beds are accessible for study because they've been exposed to the atmosphere by geological processes and deep mining projects. A severely limiting factor to deep fossil excavations is temperature, since below Earth's surface the temperature increases around 72 degrees for every mile closer to the Asthenosphere.

Another limiting factor deals with the sheer volume of rock and dirt to sift through; Measuring roughly 220.5 million cubic miles, determined by examining the global average of land mass with a thickness set to only a mile deep, which is a small fraction of the amount of existing land mass. The kicker is, many fossil excavation areas are averaging around a couple hundred meters below sea level, leaving around 87.5 percent of a proposed mile depth of crust completely unexplored.

Of course, it's completely understandable, and reasonable paleontologists couldn't tear up the Earth's crust up to a mile down without disrupting the world's ecology in a globally disastrous project. Perhaps one day though, advances in technology will help to accurately pinpoint the really deep fossils, without having to rip apart the land in the process. In which case, we may potentially discover that our ancestors had much more to worry about in daily life than what current fossil record indicates.

Provided the most accurate way to date dinosaur bones is through uranium and potassium isotopes, and not Carbon-14, this gives nearly 63.5 million years difference between ancient human fossils and dinosaur fossils. It becomes very difficult to accept humans lived with dinosaurs when looking at these numbers without sufficient evidence to fill in the gaps. Unless of course, human species really date back much older than any skeletal evidence ever found, or that a few populations of dinosaurs survived a global extinction event and then proceeded to survive for another 63.5 million years in time to live with people.; Or dating methods using these techniques are simply inaccurate for both humans and dinosaurs.

Some archaeologists are skeptical over claims one catastrophe actually wiped out all dinosaurs as we know it. This brings about questions regarding which ancient animals survived through it, where did they go, and where can evidence to prove it be found. Certain artistic works of ancient cultures seem to portray the last known time periods when a few remaining dinosaurs lived long enough to see humans, and ancient mythologies of dragons add further notion to the concept. Our ancestors clearly described dragons as we currently describe dinosaurs; The question remains. Where did our ancient relatives get the idea of a dragon?

Modern theories suggest dragons were merely crafted through imagination while observing well known creatures existing at the time of our ancestors, but recent studies indicate another method is quite possibly responsible for the birth of drakons in ancient lore. Suppose our distant relatives stumbled upon the skeletal remains of a dinosaur at some point. After seeing skeletons before in their lifetime, they likely would try to determine what creature the skeleton belonged to, undoubtedly attaching a story of some sort along with it – Similar to the process of discovery modern society goes through.

Now imagine our ancestors happened to find the skeleton or skull of a carnivorous dinosaur such as the Tyrannosaurus. What kind of stories could a dinosaur skull inspire to our ancestors? The Ica stones and other artistic works depicting dinosaurs may truly be depictions of real dinosaurs, except based on their skeletal form instead of the flesh.

It's a theory that inadvertently connects several dots across the board and can be corroborated not only in dragon specific mythologies, but also in the mythologies of other creatures too. Theorists believe ancient discoveries of dinosaur fossils inspired legends of ogres and griffins, and the same may also hold true for dragons. Official taxonomy of dinosaurs only began in the 19th century - Animals whom these bones belonged to could only be imagined prior to the class separation.

J.C. Vintner

Figures of Sitio Barriles

There is an unspoken code amongst ancient mysteries researchers in the pursuit of truth of mankind's past. It's one of honor and respect, to be open to new ideas and concepts, to be accepting of the fact history books may need to be rewritten. An incredible wealth of general research is performed around the world on a daily basis which lends to us the suggestion of something more, something beyond anything history has taught civilizations throughout the ages. Archeology and studies of human history only recently found shape within the last couple hundred years; Is it possible we perceive gaps in our history simply because these fields of research are new in the time-line due to the fact we just haven't yet found the correct knowledge to fill them in?

Recently found locations such as Sitio Barriles (the site of barrels BU-24) in Panama are great examples of ancient civilizations modern archeology knows very little of. Carbon dating suggests the site to be anywhere from 2,600 to 600 years old and hints of who inhabited the area have been discovered. The area was first studied in the 1940's although findings of the time were not published conclusively.

Artifacts found here are suggested by some archaeologists to depict deities with an eagle head, but upon further examination they appear to be something more. Figurines and pottery found embedded into rock-sides suggest the site was used for ceremonial purposes due to ash remains found in vessels believed to be used for cremation.

Characteristics of Barriles pottery and figures show a distinct Central American influence, it's sometimes thought the culture(s) who inhabited the area descended from the Maya or Inca. After many years of study, whomever lived at Sitio Barriles hundreds of years ago remains a mystery.

It's interesting to note several glyph-type carvings found throughout the area which appear to be primitive in nature, theoretically act as a type of road map to help whoever once lived there find their way around the area. The drawings take on serpent-like forms, some say to show twisting, winding paths throughout the site. When simply looking at these findings one can't help but notice the 'eagle' headed figures look more lizard, amphibian, or serpent in nature which coincides with navigation rock paintings scattered around the site.

These deities definitely take on a strange alien-like appearance. Sitio Barriles is another example of a mysterious location we know little about yet it features artifacts that tell us another, unknown ancient culture believed in hybrid deities, enough to depict them throughout the majority of remains discovered at the site.

Amalgamated

Descriptions of Bigfoot often give the impression of a part man part ape creature, coincidentally suggesting an idea of hybridization between beast and man. Researchers openly say it themselves, maybe without realizing, another possibility to its existence as a tall ape with human-like features. Hybrid beings, like Bigfoot, are found throughout the world and are actually commonplace in most cultural belief systems. Whether hybridization is between humans and animals, humans and gods, or gods and animals, ancient beliefs often touch upon these beings as those with extraordinary abilities.

Likely one of the more famous examples of hybrid amalgamations is the Cynocephali, a human with the head of a dog. Egyptians worshiped them as Anubis, Set, Horus and Hapi. Greek mythology references hybrids in the appearance of many demigods such as Centaurs, Minotaurs, Medusa, Satyrs, Cupid, Harpies, and Sirens. St. Christopher is depicted with the head of a dog in Eastern Orthodox Churches; Buddhist missionary Hui-Sheng once identified an island of dog-headed men in ancient Chinese history, which some say refers to modern Japan or North America. Bastet, Egyptian goddess part human part feline, similar to lioness Wadjet-Bast.

A statue carved by an unknown culture was discovered in a 2,600 year old archaeological site called Sitio Barriles, located in Panama; It appears to be half woman half frog (or bird), nursing a child showing the same hybridization. The list continues on as if several cultures around the world all witnessed the same beings, or a centralized culture maintained the belief which was then spread to other cultures as human population expanded. Cynocephali and animal hybrid mythologies are merely scratching the surface when it comes to how many hybrid human references exist in historical record alone.

Researchers examining ancient accounts of human animal hybridization find it difficult to ignore striking similarities between the demigods and how they're portrayed by various ancient civilizations. Usually these types of hybrids are depicted as a human body with the head of an animal, be it a raven or dog, prominent enough to focus a viewer's attention directly to the head.

In many cases it's the artwork composition which appears to be purposefully arranged in such a fashion that lines of design and contrast differential draw the onlooker exactly to these points. If the artworks could be vocalized, hybrid animal heads would be screaming at the top of their lungs while detracting viewers from other parts of the composition; Precisely depicting a level of importance even beyond that of some of the pharaohs of the time.

All hybrid beings share the same distinguished features as all animal life on the planet in the form of facial characteristics. Eyes, nose and mouth create the foundation. In essence, all walks of life are organized in a similar fashion which effectively triggers instinctual recognition upon sight. Even modern hybridization depictions by the entertainment industry tends to be associated with super natural human abilities with distinct human-like facial qualities. Science understands facial recognition phenomena as a key survival trait not only for humans, but they have also found some animals exhibiting the same capability.

Certain species of fish like the Foureye Butterflyfish for example, have color pigmentation in an eye shape near the tail fin believed to cause predatory confusion over which end should be attacked. Foureye predators usually target the eyes first, demonstrating a dependence on partial face recognition, and the Butterflyfish has developed an evolutionary trait to further its survival. This idea of a false eye plays on a phenomena known as Pareidolia, whereby significant meaning can be derived by viewing various forms and shapes resembling facial structure. Face perception is a rudimentary component for both human and animal life to a point which any hybrid concoction likely will mimic these characteristics.

Depictions of amalgamated humans have long been a part of our history and it seems the advent of modern technology is beginning to thrust this concept back into the mainstream once again. For hundreds of years half human creatures remained those of myth and ancient gods, but now machines and computers have effectively introduced a revolution of improvements to the human form. People have long been advocates of self-improvement on levels beyond natural ability, easily identified by looking at ancient uses of weapon technologies, as even a bow and arrow extends human ability to kill from a distance.

A scientific movement called Transhumanism seeks to improve natural capabilities of mankind through the use of technology while adhering to spiritual and ethical concerns of society. Sci-Fi brought about the idea as cyborgs, exemplified by works such as the Bionic Man, featuring part electrical machine humanoids with extraordinary abilities beyond run of the mill blessings of nature. Interestingly, several people around the world have already started human machine hybridization with such devices as the pacemaker and bionic limbs. Recent break-through studies have created working computer software programs capable of mouse interactions using nothing more than thought stimulation. Ironically, cyborg technologies seem to be running parallels with our ancient past, to improve upon the human form, for the benefit of our future survival.

A physical joining of humans and machines in the form of bionics may not be the only way ancient hybrids came into play according to some theorists. When examining the same ancient deities, new age researchers started to notice a link between modern genetic experiments and hybridization evidence of the past, suggesting the possibility our ancestors may have manipulated DNA themselves or with the aid of alien technology, if not performed animal-human transplant surgeries.

Evidently, mainstream science and archeology disagree on his point of view and consider ancient reliefs as nothing more than artistic renditions of deities. However, science of today is attempting to solve countless riddles of the human genome in an effort to improve life quality by means of genetic manipulation, undoubtedly something of prominent interest to our ancient ancestors. Profound curiosities such as the Fountain of Youth, Emerald Tablet of Hermes, and Elixir of Life help corroborate mankind's quest to live eternally.

There are countless scriptures referring to the very same principal. Maybe it's possible ancient hybrids reflect a similar idea, to combine beneficial qualities of animal life with humans, in order to create superior god-like beings capable of advancing humanity by living forever.

There are few eyewitness accounts in the past hundred years referring specifically to types of hybrid humans only previously considered as part of ancient Greek mythology. Satyr related sightings like the Lake Worth Monster and Maryland Goatman are eerily reminiscent in description of typical characters played in Greek play-write Aeschylus' masterpieces. Unlike Greek mythologies, modern Satyrs aren't reported to be carrying instruments or playing music, although habitats and physical characteristics do seem to match up.

Aside from a a few encounters, half man half goat creatures occasionally show up in mainstream movies and cartoons, maintaining their typical surreal presence over the years. While some are portrayed as peaceful music loving hybrid spirits of nature, their cloven hooves meet association commonly with the devil and his minions as popularized by Shakespeare, being a sign of evil themselves accompanied with horns. Goats are known for extraordinary climbing abilities, reaching areas where humans may never set foot even as an accomplished rock climber.

A great example of goat death-defying feats can be found at the Cingino Dam, Italy. The Alpine Ibex living here have adapted to scale a 160 ft. near vertical man-made structure without really breaking a sweat. In fact, most of the Ibex at Cingino appear comfortable and safe, likely because they know predators can't reach them. Traits of Ibex, and other fantastic climbing goats, fall into a category of abilities which humans definitely would enjoy sharing. Imagine being able to climb sheer cliffs effortlessly, maintain stable footing no matter the terrain, and carry forth a respectable set of defensive horns, all while retaining many benefits of being human.

Unexplained Flying Creatures

Spending thousands of years hiding in caves from predatory attacks eventually takes its toll on the psyche. Threats came from above and on land during the cave era, it was absolutely vital to find safe shelter to ensure survival in a much wilder world than we know today. People must have been on constant alert all waking hours, with some staying awake on shift intervals during the night, even with fire and weapons. They had to do it, there was no other choice. Relaxation as it is today most likely was a very rare event for life during the ancient ages as survival remained constantly on the line.

Predatory danger could strike without a moment's notice and we understand our ancestors must have unfortunately learned this the hard way. Still they fought through and found ways not only to cope with being hunted, but to become the better hunter in tactic, by passing down knowledge for future generations. Information needed a way of living on even when our ancestors didn't. They drew teachings on cave walls just as we doodle notes on the refrigerator for family, except our ancestors faced the likelihood of death to wild animals on a daily basis. There was always the chance of not coming home from a trip for water, to forage, or during a daring hunt. Telling these stories more often became critically dependent on using visual imagery to stimulate the imagination; A great way to teach understanding considering the unpredictable nature of situations in the wild.

Large birds in a role of significance and power are often mentioned in ancient Indian texts, as an example. The Island of Java's historical record indicates population began around 6,000 years ago. For many years Java was caught in a tussle as cultures from around the world tried to claim its territory. The Mongols, Portuguese, Spanish, British, Dutch and Japanese all fought for the island until Indonesia was granted independence in the mid 20th century.

Although influenced by several different cultures, Javanese hold roots in East Indian mythology and lore. The Iban of Borneo, who migrated from China to Indonesia, believe Sengalang Burong is the origin of creation and lives throughout the forests of Java. Accepted translation of Sengalang Burong in English means the bird chief or bird god, aptly fitting Iban religious beliefs as all birds being the manifestation of the spirit son of Burong. Further tracing the lore we find that Sengalang himself manifests as a white and brown hawk. Interestingly, Javanese Wood Owls currently living on the island are also white and brown, with hawk-like features.

In the late 1920's naturalist Dr. Ernest Bartels entered part of the forest locals claimed he should not go based on spiritual beliefs. He ended up having a close encounter with a giant bird as it flew over his head and later referenced what happened, calling this bird an Ahool, after the unique howling sound it let out while passing by. Ivan Sanderson confirmed later, by Bartels' account and an encounter of his own, that it must be a new species. Both visitors claimed local residents of the island knew of very large flying creatures in the rain-forest, but generally elected to stay away themselves. Since large species of Earless owls exist in the Javanese forest, it both aids and hinders Bartels' case at the same time.

It's quite possible an unknown subspecies exists with gray fur and very rarely witnessed, and on the other hand, researchers might believe based on details of Bartels' encounters that he simply confronted one of the Earless owl species; Possibly a specimen with melatonin deficiency causing feathers to lose pigment.

A plausible explanation for both Ernest and Ivan's events could very well be mistaken identity, and a very close encounter as described might result in the Ahool-type noise heard due to a Doppler effect from a territorial protective Earless owl. There is of course a third possibility,

349

that Ernest and Ivan may have encountered the bird god Sengalang Burong, and the very reason locals would not enter those parts of the forest.

Ancestral history through oral tradition is an effective method for passing down knowledge from generation to generation in many cultures around the world. Transforming important lessons, dangers, and healthful knowledge into easy to remember stories using association techniques helps commit ideas to memory, making it less likely to be forgotten over long periods of time. North American Indian culture without doubt is a great example of this practice as evident in countless legends and mythologies.

One of the most famous Indian legends details a giant bird some believe might be a reference to a pterodactyl through many descriptions of the bird's prominent features and behaviors. Studying this legend further has brought an entirely different perspective, something that demonstrates the true nature of learning a valuable lesson, and passing it to others, as a warning of danger. In essence, this legend details a bird so powerful it can create thunderstorms as it moves throughout the sky. The Thunderbird is a spirit not to be reckoned with; Examining his origin story reveals an intriguing message carried on throughout the years.

It begins with two Indians traveling north to discover exactly where thunder comes from. They encounter a very high mountain with darting clefts closing in on each other rather quickly. One of the Indians, named Passamaquoddies, told the other to continue looking for the place thunder comes from if he didn't survive the cleft. Passamaquoddies passed over the cleft without a problem but his friend did not. He continued on his way, looking for the origin of thunder, and found a group of Indians playing a ball game.

The group of Indians, perhaps startled, ran into their wigwams and came out with wings, equipped with bows and arrows, and flew south over the mountain. Passamaquoddies believed he found the Thunderbird's home, he confronted elders in the camp for help. They discussed how they may help and did so by placing Passamaquoddies in a giant mortar; crushing his bones into the shape of a Thunderbird, after which he was given wings, a bow, and arrows.

The elders told him fly away but not too close to trees as they would kill him. Passamaquoddies became the Thunderbird. He tried to leave and was confronted by Wochowsen (the Wind Blower and rival), who placed a strong wind in his path. Glooscap (the creator) seen this happening and broke Wochowsen's wings to halt the winds and let Passamaquoddies pass. After some time Glooscap noticed the broken wings of Wochowsen caused the air not to move, the waters to become stagnant, and the fish to die; So he repaired Wochowsen's wings just enough to moderate winds and bring life back to Wochowsen's people.

Tracing elements of this creation legend brought about interesting details which paint an alternative meaning to the story, providing practical reasons for why this myth is important to the respective people; A few key details here help build a more accurate purpose. Traditional Indian beliefs cite that spirits fly close to heavens with the gods in the form of birds. Wigwams, referred to by Passamaquoddies, are traditionally found in the American Northeast which helps narrow down a location to where the event described might have taken place.

The next clue is in the reference of Glooscap, known as The Creator to the Penobscot Nation, who live in the American Northeast in Maine and New Brunswick. Searching the Appalachians in the Northeast area between Maine and New Brunswick brings us to Mount Katahdin. This mountain was named by the Penobscot Indians, meaning The Greatest Mountain.

One summit to Mount Katahdin, called the Knife's Edge, is a more dangerous travel point along the Appalachians with a 483 meter long section only 3 foot wide between steep drop-offs on each side. Perhaps this is where Passamaquoddies and his friend ventured to find clefts quickly closing in the search for the source of thunder.

If this is the case, the legend of the Thunderbird might have an entirely different meaning altogether. The story could translate to this - An Indian and his friend traveling into the dangerous mountains during a windy period; Passamaquoddies made it back home after the wind finally calmed down, after seeing the place where Thunderbirds live, but without his friend. The elders question his actions. He explains the journey to the top of the mountain, that he found the place of the spirits, and wished to find the source of thunder.

They debate Passamaquoddies' wish carefully and eventually granted bravery by giving him death, so that he may fly with the other spirits to find thunder's origin. It's quite possible Passamaquoddies requested this in order to avenge his friend's death, and to warn others about dangers of the mountain for generations to come. If this is the case, then the story of the

Thunderbird becomes a myth with a much deeper meaning, transformed into a legend for future generations of Penobscot Indians to hold close in their hearts by oral tradition.

Warning of danger sometimes proves to be futile like recounting a story of the boy who cried wolf. Ideas of pleasantries might need to be saved as attribution to an eventual outcome as opposed to the controversial history of a small town called Point Pleasant once burdened by a similar tale. Long before the Silver Bridge collapse and paranormal events leading to it, Point Pleasant was Fort Randolph, site of the first engagement of the American Revolution. Two rivers meet at this sublime point, the Kanawha and Ohio. Kanawha River became known by multiple names as fights emerged over disputed territory.

The French attempted to capture Fort Randolph without success, naming the river Tchadakoin. Preceding the Battle of Point Pleasant, the Iroquois aptly named these two rivers, Chautauqua, referring appropriately as two moccasins tied together. It was the Iroquois land, to the south and east of the Ohio river signed over to the English, as responsible for initial conflict between English settlers and the Mingo, and a few Delaware Indians.

The Mingo were known at the time for being controversial and feisty, they tried pushing English settlers off Indian land, to the other side of the Appalachians. Shawnee Chief Cornstalk attempted to procure peace after leading his people into a strong English resistance ending in stalemate. Very few Shawnee tribe members were in agreement with Mingo and Delaware actions but followed Cornstalk into battle.

According to record, Chief Cornstalk was killed by an English soldier on his way to peace talks and buried on site. Legend claims Cornstalk uttered the words of an everlasting curse of the Great Spirit on the area during his last dying breaths, which some believe is the true reason for strange events happening in Point Pleasant since.

One of the more prominent occurrences of unexplained phenomena grabbed media attention in the late 1960s when several residents began reporting sightings of a giant bird-like man. Skeptics deciphering descriptions from reports believe witnesses fabricated the creature, mostly due to erroneous circumstances.

Biology researchers analyzing the case would say The Mothman, as locals named it, must be a Sandhill Crane or some sort of large Heron. Word passed around town with a common belief this grayish skinned moth creature lived in an abandoned World War II dynamite factory.

Talks eventually spun out of control, perhaps in fear or panic, to incorporate the biological explanation, claiming a large bird mutated from exposure to toxic wastes while hiding at the factory. It was even proposed TNT chemical contamination in a nearby wildlife refuge may have been altering perception of local residents by seeping into the water supply and animal game, causing the mind to distort occurrences which otherwise may be completely natural.

A controversial photograph showing a large dark figure clinging to the top of a support on the Silver Bridge seemed to corroborate witness testimonies. Stories, rumors and paranormal type activity escalated until one moment, when the Silver Bridge collapsed, sending forty people into the river below. According to many folk in Point Pleasant the Mothman occurrences stopped after this point.

Locals started thinking due to this connection, that perhaps the Mothman was trying to warn of danger before it happened, but the significance was not realized until it was too late. Later, it was found after an extensive structural investigation, the apparent cause of the bridge's failure was due to an accidental micro-fracture in a connecting piece created during the manufacturing process.

Originally the Silver Bridge held a light amount of traffic and vehicle weight, but over the years it increased all the while gradually increasing the metal fracture's size. The devastation in Point Pleasant became a blessing to other parts of the United States as the event triggered creation of a national bridge inspection organization responsible for examining bridge safety on a regular basis. It is unfortunate such events have to occur in order to save the lives of people in the future, but perhaps this may have been Mothman's intent. Could it be possible Mothman was trying to bring awareness to an entire country over these sorts of dangers?

Shawnee history describes how the Mothman might be a combination of two different stories. Legend of Misignwa proposes the existence of a spirit protecting animals in the forest who watches hunters to see if they're being disrespectful to nature. Hunters who are disrespectful would have accidents at the hand of the Misignwa. Traditionally this spirit resembles Bigfoot more than it does Mothman by looking at ceremonial dress used during the Bread Dance; The dancer wears a full bearskin, wood mask, and holds a turtle shell rattle cane to commemorate.

However, the principal message of Misignwa legend does suggest a spirit of the forest may have been responsible for the accident at Silver Bridge, if per say hunters were disrespectful in Point Pleasant. Interestingly, this indeed might be the case. In the 1950s, Mason County Courthouse was demolished and Chief Cornstalk's remains were unearthed, likely disrupting slumber of a chief who fought until the very end for the peace of his people.

Another Shawnee legend referring to Mothman sightings of Point Pleasant may be derived from the story of White Hawk, which by a little imagination may fit the profile of Mothman to greater degree than Misignwa. In this legend, an Indian by the name of Waupee lived in the forest alone, he became intrigued by the Star Chief's daughter who lived high up in the sky.

They had a child together, but the child was brought to live in the sky instead of in the forest with Waupee; He terribly missed her and his son. One day the chief gave Waupee an option to live in the sky, but first Waupee was required to pass a test involving gathering bits of animals of the forest.

The chief said for each of the family to choose a part of an animal for that is what they'll become. Star Chief's daughter, Waupee, and their son all chose a white hawk's feather instead, to descend back to the forest.

The legend then explains the families of the white hawks continue to live in the forest. Perhaps residents of Point Pleasant witnessed apparitions of White Hawks during the events leading up to the collapse of the Silver Bridge. Whether the Mothman can be attributed to Shawnee Indian legend, an alien visitation, or something complete different, one intriguing fact remains. Point Pleasant became the center of an unknown phenomena witnessed by many locals who sincerely believe extraordinary events took place prior to an incident responsible for not only changing a town's perspective on life, but also for opening the eyes of a nation.

Otherworldly Beings & Apparitions

Belief in an alternate existence, or other-world, have long been a part of human nature. For as long as historical record traces back, and then beyond through oral tradition, mankind has constantly looked to other realms to explain our own existence. There are many reasons why anyone might find worlds beyond current reality as comforting and fulfilling. It seems we are spiritual by our existence, through our consciousness, without doubt a type of extra sensory perception to say the least. In essence humankind believes in a multitude of spiritual concepts.

From gods to deities, souls, ghosts, aliens, superstitious encounters, cryptids, unexplained, paranormal activity and supernatural events. When assessed as an entire collective, and without segregation of the masses, we find uniquely it's quite common and essential for human life on Earth to believe (on some level) of something beyond known physical realities.

Even those who support a neutral standpoint, believing in the absence of any higher level being, still have a belief system which defines them. From here we congregate by establishing relationships with others who share the same beliefs, even so far as to keep our distance and/or slander those who's beliefs are too unlike our own.

Through this process we make ourselves different even if in spirit we are the same. The broad diversity of belief systems throughout the world is largely due to cultural influence yet no matter how each culture explains our existence, the same basic principals permeate through the fabric of society. One of the more predominant concepts evident in several cultures concerns itself with an idea of life after death, often portrayed by souls or spirit entities with an ability to affect the physical world in some form or another. Where life goes after passing on is one of the greatest mysteries of being human.

Incidentally, science may corroborate spirituality in this sense by physics and the law of conservation of energy. We are made of energy, and if energy cannot be destroyed, where does our energy really go when we die? This principal can be applied to birth in asking where did the energy come from that created us? Surely the physical part of our energy is dispersed back into the environment, but that doesn't necessarily include our consciousness or soul for that matter.

There are people who truly believe they have lived past lives and maybe physics provides a practical answer in the same light. It's here, in the place where belief systems turn to suggest our spirit or soul lives on with an afterlife, sometimes manifesting in the physical realm for specific reasons that sometimes we might not fully understand. Moreover, these manifestations are practically always associated with significant events and/or specific emotional stress. The term 'haunting' is synonymous with ghostly apparitions as malevolent beings who may have met tragic ends or endured a life of trauma. Psychic mediums attest certain spirits may act in this fashion in a means to resolve unfinished business in a previous life, to avenge those who brought the spirits harm in the first place, and fortunately not all ghosts come across in this manor.

Some apparitions said to bring about positive change, who warn of imminent danger, and attempt to protect loved ones who still walk the Earth. It's acceptable to say, with the possibility of spirits being our lives after death, these actions adhere to a similar code of conduct people carry out on a regular basis during life; So long as interpretations of ghostly beings and their motives aren't imposed subliminally as an extension of human psyche.

Beliefs of some people may say nothing exists after life and once we die, it's the end to everything, even so bold to say we do nothing more than fill space in the meantime. In a way this is an unfortunate outlook on life, to say we essentially live our life for a period of time and then disappear forever without a trace beyond the dust our bodies have left behind. Consciousness and emotions hint to us constantly, they're trying to tell us there is more to life. Science continuously needs to correct its theories simply because new ideas and concepts of life are always being discovered. Every time one question is answered, thousands follow.

Our existence is deeper than black holes are mysterious and there's no telling how capable we might be as an advanced civilization even hundreds of years from now. Cultures around the world have believed in extraordinary ability, in the possibility of life existing elsewhere in the cosmos, that there is more meaning to life than what meets the eye. These concepts define us as human, define us as something beyond simplistic day to day survival, and are rooted deeply inside our spiritual existence. We have been given these gift and it would be a shame not to explore each one to its fullest perceivable potential. Life could easily exist outside of Earth by mathematics alone; It would be a waste of space otherwise, as Carl Sagan would assure us. The same applies to how we see life on an everyday basis. If we think our consciousness ends when we die, then it sure would be a waste of spiritual intelligence.

Maybe it's possible life moves to alternate realms at death, and the event of dying happens in a way which signifies our transfer of energy into another dimension. Near death experiences have gathered a name for themselves as many thousands of people find this mysterious existence each year. They report euphoria, calming sensations, out of body experiences, tunnels of purely white light, psychic phenomena, and much more. For what reason? Science can track these events down to how electricity is manipulated in the brain, how it may tamper with memories, and alter people's personalities. Yet right now, it cannot tell us from a spiritual perspective what the events truly mean or why they change lives so profoundly. Often thoughts of NDE's are reminder to some of how they once caught a glimpse into the future and learned how life might be for them in years to follow.

Premonitions can be shocking at first when trying to deal with their ground shaking, anxiety building significance. For years they may seem purely as coincidences until it happens more and more, in ways which tell the mind, this is the truth of reality - For what's been, is now happening. In a few cases people who experience near death scenarios do report the presence of otherworldly beings with no real understanding of what they mean. Personal interpretations of these situations will touch upon spiritual belief, claiming the unknown entities must be part of the afterlife in some way.

A very similar phenomena is reported commonly among alien abduction cases, whereby people encounter unknown beings, shadows, and shapes of entities during the event. Unlike NDE reports, abductions often focus on experimentation toward the subject, at times in a very helpless and horrific manor. Psychologists and Hypnotherapists have studied these phenomena extensively, they too have trouble (as their patients) to understand why it happens; Especially when they examine healthy individuals without any sort of preexisting condition. Some scientists believe the abduction phenomena can simply be attributed to a combination of mass influence and traumatic life events, yet believers have a very different outlook from the experience.

Perhaps what people witness during these strange encounters, in combination with cryptid creatures, is an example of afterlife spirits or entities from another realm attempting to make contact with us. Suppose we visited a distant planet in the universe with life flourishing upon the surface, and suppose that life was at the same point in scientific evolution as ourselves. Going a step even further, imagine the species living on that world shared similar biological characteristics to our own. How would they react seeing us for the first time? Possibly slight variances in biological makeup would have us appear similar yet different enough, and the travel method to reach their planet may affect the space-time continuum, thus altering our appearance even more.

Apprehension tags along with human travel to distant reaches of the universe and with it follows precautionary methods of exploration. Reconnaissance is necessary, drone devices become even more helpful, and new types of safe guards yet to be invented could change the playing field before any human is put into potentially dangerous situations.

For example, developing a holographic reconnaissance vehicle capable of collecting environment data could be used to test the waters. Perhaps such a vehicle is shaped similar to biological life forms re-con cameras picked up from the distance in order to find out first-hand what level of threat might be encountered - *Reminiscent of some Bigfoot reports, where the apparent creature vanishes completely when shot at.*

Safe exploration tactics will rely on the art of deception, to blend with foreign environments and any biological life present. Psychology definitely plays a role here and every last drop of intelligence can mean the difference between a successful encounter or a detrimental one.

What if by chance this scenario is already happening here on Earth? Some researchers believe foreign reconnaissance from distant parts of the universe has played a significant role in shaping human history. They believe apparitions, spirit entities, cryptid sightings, UFOs, crop circles and more, are all part of elaborate missions to determine whether or not humanity is able to cope with face to face encounters from other worlds. Of course, foreign life forms likely would need to exhibit an insurmountable level of patience to deal with spontaneous human reaction to the unknown, if this is indeed the case.

Quantum Cryptids

An experiment in the late 1970's helped bolster revolutionary views of Einstein's principal theories in physics by examining the path of a photon through a double-slit apparatus. According to Einstein, light exists as both a wave and particle at the same moment in time. In 1978, John Wheeler set out to determine the state of a photon during an observation process, be it a wave or a particle, influenced by human thought. The basic idea is that if an observer knows which slit the photon would travel through, predicting its path, it remains in the particle state.

If an observer was unaware of the possible outcome, the photon would turn enter a wave state, capable of affecting its own path. Wheeler proved in these thought experiments a strange property of physics whereby light is seemingly capable of affecting itself in the past, from a future state. Further studies by colleagues after Wheeler's demonstrations eventually confirmed his findings. In theory these delayed choice experiments reaffirm particles can exist in two states at once which can be influenced through observation.

The idea also purposes an enhanced capability of human subconscious or an altered state of which it can exist. A specific distraction to our consciousness allows the subconscious to act through itself without preconceived influence or notion, thus allowing subconscious to manifest its own acceptable realities.

Sounds quite complicated really. What it seems to indicate is the human mind may very well be capable of influencing past realities simply by the nature of its mechanism. Quantum physics suggests the past, present and future all coexist, and that affecting any state of time will equally affect the others. Humans know premeditated choices of the present can change the future, changing the past incidentally once the chosen future has passed. What's yet to be proven by physics is whether or not we are capable of modifying past events from the present state even though theory suggests it to be true. Perhaps it requires a long series of micro adjustments to build one larger past observed by all conscious histories - If enough people believe, will it happen?

In the event people are capable of changing their past by observing it differently, we begin to notice how encounters with cryptid beings and spiritual apparitions could take form as manifestations the subconscious believes to exist, alerting the conscious mind to their presence. It could explain why human artifacts have been discovered in places which seem otherwise impossible by current perception. Fossilized footprints, modern tools embedded in ancient rocks, nails and bullets entrapped in amber. All explainable by a proposed strange and twisted ability of human conscious to affect our past beyond comprehension.

Perhaps this concept might also explain conditions such as sleep paralysis which in extreme cases can produce out of body experiences lasting for hours. People experiencing sleep paralysis report seeing shadowy intruders, describing them in a very similar fashion to hostile alien abduction stories without the experimentation aspect. Witnessing odd figures during the incidents are often accompanied with a strong pressure on the chest, or a general feeling the entity is pinning the person down. Science has a decent understanding as far as how sleep paralysis affects neurons in the brain and knows of a few catalysts responsible for invoking the condition. The realm linking human conscious to these events remains largely unexplored beyond that of stress or environmental factors.

Ancient lore in at least ten cultures associates night paralysis specifically with demon encounters. They tend to believe an alternate realm or spiritual place is attempting to communicate with them during sleep, and in some cases this means a deceased relative trying to relay important information. Often the event is frightening to observers, who believe they're truly witnessing an alternative reality, pinning them into a helpless position. This feeling would be terrifying to anyone awake in the middle of the day, left with full body paralysis unexpectedly, only able to move their eyes. It's quite possible paralytic episodes provide a glimpse into the mind's stimulated creation process.

To some researchers it may indicate a reoccurring fear of subconscious meeting a person's conscious realm in physical form. As with photons, traveling both in wave and particle forms, the subconscious and conscious may exhibit a similar behavior. When the subconscious is observed with known intent of its destination, a particle state is retained. If subconscious is indirectly observed without it being aware of the observation, it retains a wave state. Ultimately suggesting from a quantum principal that the human brain operates by both particles and waves, at the same instant in time. Meaning, studying a person's brain wave patterns is only revealing half of what might really be happening.

Coupling quantum physics with the idea of legendary cryptids witnessed around the world provides a different theory explaining their existence. A possibility suggesting people are capable of manifesting creatures and apparitions by indirectly focusing their own energy, or by channeling subconscious behavior through indirect observation. Perhaps as technology advances, brain capacity slowly expands. Spiritual encounters continue to increase as the human brain becomes more sensitive to alternate dimensions and previously undiscovered realms. In the case which our spirits may indeed live on eternally, as an extension of energy granted to us by the cosmos, we may one day be able to fluidly access these hidden areas of life.

Wildman & Bigfoot

Undoubtedly one of the most famous, legendary cryptids around the world has to be Bigfoot by in part to countless eyewitness reports, video evidence, foot prints, audio clips, and even DNA findings. The amount of sightings and fragmented evidence suggesting some type of tall hairy humanoid creature exists out there is truly overwhelming. Probably a huge factor in Squatch popularity is what exactly this sort of discovery means to mankind on multiple levels. Their resemblance to humans is striking in many ways - Imagine if the Sasquatch population turned out to actually be our living ancestors!

Although the name Bigfoot is traditionally attributed to the North American area, we find numerous accounts of near identical creatures roaming the wild in other parts of the globe; Each area tends to have its own specific native name (and lore) used for referring to these creatures. It comes to no surprise for many trackers and researchers attempting to make the physical discovery that Bigfoots do exist considering evolution of human population alone.

Our ancient ancestors branched off from their origins in Africa to settle the world over. Many contributing factors may suggest how

Sasquatch is indeed part of our species, breaking off from mainstream groups to survive away from society.

Descriptions of the legendary cryptid, Bigfoot, point to a confusing mixture between Homo habilis and Homo erectus (approximately 0.5-2 million years ago) mainly due to the fact that sightings always indicate a completely hairy biped with ape-like features, wearing no clothing, and often alone. Archaeological record demonstrates our ancestors did not begin to live in groups or wear clothing until the Neanderthal age, around 30-100 thousand years ago. The record also portrays a transition period when both Cro-Magnon and Neanderthal coexisted, just as Cro-Magnon and Homo sapiens later in the time-line. Mixed traits between the latest two have even been discovered in Portugal, dating to nearly 25,000 years ago.

As our ancestors spread around the globe, and started to live in groups together, it doesn't seem out of the ordinary that some of them may have split off during these transition phases. Suppose part of Homo erectus population continued on by themselves during formation of the Neanderthal period, deciding not to wear clothing or live in larger groups, or simply that they were too far away from the groups to pickup this evolutionary change.

Since Homo erectus survived on the planet for nearly 1.5 million years, according to fossil record, it's not unreasonable to think they could somehow survive another 300,000 years into present day; After all, anatomically modern humans known today are believed to have emerged 200,000 years ago.

Encounter reports often include distinct features which transcend the testimonies of thousands of eyewitnesses around the world; No matter the location, there are elements to Bigfoot sightings that always remain consistent just like the phenomena of alien abduction reports.

Usually the creature reported is bipedal, standing between 7 to 10 foot tall, has a large muscular frame, prominent ape-like features, covered in hair, and sometimes (more often than not) a strong foul odor permeates through the air. At times Squatch are known to throw rocks, knock on wood, arrange twigs or feathers in parallel patterns, and vocalize their presence.

The height range is commonly claimed as falsified by matter of approximation for humans encountering something under duress, but this too is not unreasonable to expect when examining our history. A taller subspecies of humans isn't a new concept. Giants decorated pages folklore for thousands of years and might even be in relation to evolutionary responses to environmental change.

Archaeologists recently discovered proof evolutionary response on the opposite end of the spectrum. Hobbit sized humans, now known as Homo floresiensis, lived approximately 18,000 years ago on a remote island of Indonesia. Scientists believe their pygmy size can be attributed to evolutionary adaptation, from being isolated in a small island environment over thousands of years. If the environment can impact the height of a living creature as such, then it's not out of the question that Bigfoot is a similar adaptation to the environments it's known to inhabit.

Certain species of domesticated fish and plants make a great example of how environmental constraints can limit growth proportions. When the fish tank or plant pot is too small compared to biological growth potential, the plant or fish will only grow to a size relative to the container. Once the same fish or plant is moved to a larger container able to sustain maximum growth, biological growth can then continue as if not limited.

This environmental constraint is even evident in current human population. People living in less dense populations are on average taller than those living in more densely populated areas. If these cryptids really are part of a continued line of Homo erectus, perhaps living in large forests and marshy areas for thousands of years contributed to specific genetic changes, resulting in a larger forest adapted type of human we call, Bigfoot.

Some theories also propose Sasquatch are actually just misidentified modern humans who removed themselves from mainstream society to live in the woods sometime within the last few thousand years. New age theorists even propose the possibility of people living in current society defecting into the wild to be free of their burdens and free from the demands of modern life. There are few notable examples of such individuals. We know it happens, rarely, but we don't know exactly how many times it happens. A problem with this theory is trying to explain how AWOL folk continue to survive so evasively, and exactly how modern people could take on the appearance of Bigfoot in a seemingly short time.

One idea considers how domesticated pigs quickly develop a thick fur, grow tusks, and revert to primitive survival traits when left in the wild, incidentally becoming fully environmentally efficient in just a few short generations. This transformation for humans is largely unknown to modern science, and the majority of what we do know is thanks to those few individuals who have tried it with public knowledge only to meet an unfortunate end. It also doesn't take into consideration common details from Sasquatch sightings such as being 7 foot tall, leaving large foot prints and sometimes traces of unknown DNA in hair samples.

Another hypothesis points to a rare condition called Hypertrichosis which causes abnormal hair growth over the entire body. Stephan Bibrowski was one of the more famous people with this ailment, growing hair up to eight inches thick over his face and around four inches thick around his body. Bibrowski performed in the circus making the best of his condition, but unfortunately people who are affected by Hypertrichosis do not always have this type of reaction. Certain legends in Europe claim werewolves are real people affected by the syndrome, living out in the wild, taking their revenge on society for its ridicule.

This idea is often confronted by the rarity retort of Hypertrichosis, saying it's very unlikely to be a plausible explanation for the number of incidents involving werewolves. However, it does lend merit to ideas of wild humans roaming the backwoods, suggesting once again that humans might be indirectly responsible for Sasquatch sightings. In the Himalayas they are sometimes referred to as wild men, man bears, or jungle men aside from the coined term of Yeti.

Part way around the world, in North American Shawnee Indian tradition, the Misignwa is a spirit living in the forest who protects any animals in its vicinity and will cause misfortune to disrespectful hunters. Misignwa are represented during an annual Bread Dance as a human dressed in bearskin with a wooden mask, carrying a cane and turtle shell rattle.

Science requires conclusive evidence to separate fact from legend which in this case might be biological evidence, fossilized remains, or even a living specimen. With Bigfoot, eyewitness testimony only provides an interesting viewpoint for a case and not enough for verdict. As Carl Sagan once said, we must concede that: If you never looked for evidence, or if you wouldn't have found it even if you looked, then the absence of evidence isn't evidence of anything. Perhaps the fossil record does not indicate the presence of Homo erectus in the last 300,000 years simply because we haven't found the right places to look. There are a multitude of factors of why archeology continues to find gaps in biological time-lines especially considering the ever-changing dynamic of our world. The fact is: All over the world people are reporting sightings of large human-like creatures dwelling in the backwoods of civilization.

More recently have these sightings been taken to the next level with trained professional field biologists discovering unknown DNA evidence, highly suggesting the existence of a previously undiscovered species. To many scientists the idea of Bigfoot is far-fetched but not completely ruled out, usually met with a skeptic approach saying if they did exist, we would know about it by now. In all honesty, such a statement is closed-minded, lacks imagination, and is very repressive to aspiring scientists.

Explaining eyewitness testimonies may not be easy, but this evidence is enough to warrant full scale investigations as the BFRO and other organizations are performing to find and/or capture a Sasquatch themselves. Since these Sasquatch are very elusive, maybe it might be wise to tag and track, instead of hauling it in live or dead for studies. Radio tags, maybe even miniature video transmitters could tell us much more about behavior, living conditions, and survival in the wild.

Largely contesting existence of Bigfoot by skeptics are questions which ask why it's too difficult to find any biological remains of the creature. There are a few probable answers beyond typical responses if indeed Bigfoot is in the line of Homo erectus. Generally field researchers quickly counter a lack of bone remains is due to scavengers, or decay rates of matter on a dense forest floor. Of course these are plausible explanations but they're geared to looking at Bigfoot strictly as some sort of wild animal. When we look at Bigfoot as a Homo erectus, or Homo habilis, we find a different story altogether.

According to some anthropologists, cannibalism dates to early periods of human history which is partially corroborated by archaeological evidence found in ancient Neanderthal remains. This dates to after the habilis and erectus period yet doesn't necessarily mean it wasn't practiced before then too. There are many reasons for cannibalistic practices that often centralized spiritual belief and these acts also happened in times of severe hunger in order to survive. Among techniques discovered for this practice we find at least two that could contribute to a lack in Bigfoot remains if funerary cannibalism is part of their survival.

Burial and bone crushing, both of which leave little structural elements behind to indicate they were once bones, much too obscure to be found commonly in thick forests. Burial seems to be the more likely scenario of the two, drawing even further parallel to modern human living. A third possibility could be cremation. It's not unreasonable to consider these humanoid cryptids as opportunistic, they may very well take advantage of naturally occurring fires, although open fires are extraordinarily rare in eyewitness reports as the majority of time Sasquatch appears to be in traveling mode.

To some researchers, the lack of physical remains of Sasquatch type cryptids around the world may also be an indication of something otherworldly, and more along the lines of alien encounters. In this hypothesis it's believed there must be some sort of alternative explanation for why thousands of people witness presence of Bigfoot first hand, find tracks and DNA evidence, but haven't been able to capture an actual creature. It even suggests reasoning why photographs and video footage tend to have troubles obtaining unmistakably crystal clear images.

The theory claims human-like cryptids are cross-dimensional beings who travel from another realm or dimension to visit our world for reasons we can't quite explain. Sasquatch could be observing mankind to determine an effect means of communication, or perhaps the species hasn't figured out a way to communicate with us beyond physical manifestation.

J.C. Vintner

*Maybe what eyewitness find are distorted
realities of another realm bleeding into the fabric
of our own space-time continuum.*

     Some reports give the strong indication we might be dealing with cross-dimensional beings, such as a hunter taking aim and firing at a Squatch only to see it disappear into thin air at the sound of his rifle. If indeed Bigfoot is a biological form of this planet, those are certainly the most incredible reflexes known to exist. Ultimately researchers will continue to be confronted with a heightened level of mystery until such time these profound encounters can be logically explained.

Epilogue

Discoveries continue to reshape what we know of the past. Lets say the Earth was frozen at this very moment and covered in a thick blanket of dust. How long would it take for future beings with absolutely no clue as to what a human was, discover us? How much time is necessary to figure our buried technology? Consider there is a strong possibility this purposed futuristic culture probably took a different evolutionary route. Perhaps they perfected bio-technology early on and their computers are actually self-replicating, self-generating plants which exist in harmony. Similar to our carbon dioxide feeding trees which in turn feed us with oxygen. They could look at our technology and consider the components to be nothing more than primitive artwork. Although, given the purposed scenario it's much more appropriate to believe such a culture would realize the discovered objects are not those crafted by nature. In turn this would immediately start a chain reaction of discovery to finding the meaning and ultimately leading the futuristic society into asking the same question we did thousands of years before.

To some humanity is not the first nor will be the last creation of intelligent beings. Perhaps millions of years ago a similar species existed which mastered technologies only to face its own demise by an unfortunate series of events. Maybe remnants of super ancient societies are mixed in with archaeological evidence uncovered to this day. The results could be confusing us further when trying to solve the riddle of our past for this reason. If evolution evolved once, it seems likely evolution has evolved before in other ways as it continues to evolve simultaneously on other worlds.

The point is that even-though we may not currently possess the knowledge or evidence as proof of, we are most certainly not alone in the grand scheme of things. Life on Earth is part of something unimaginably greater than any concept could ever begin to perceive. We are part of the balance of nature which exists on multiple realms and worlds throughout the entire Universe. Life scales from the microscopic to vast gigantic reaches. For all we know, we could very well be living and breeding on a cell of a much larger being beyond comprehension. As a manifestation of energy into life-form we must acknowledge and embrace life for it is the force for why we exist.

Even by scientific reasoning this holds true. To say energy can neither be created or destroyed, it is breathed into us. The same energy is passed on as we pass on into other living beings, into the environment, and into space. Exactly why many of us on Earth feel the presence of our past realities and relatives. The energy is not destroyed. It lives on as it did before we were given the gift.

By energy we are all related on a fundamental level. A blood test or DNA test is not necessary to prove all life, no matter where it might be found, is essentially related. Energy pulses through everything. Even if our culture deems a rock is not living, energy still exists within. Somewhere down the line mankind forgot what this means. It is a gap in our history, one sometimes filled by greed and selfishness.

In the bible God is mentioned to be all encompassing. To some it's taught that God can see everything they do. Why? Is the reference to the very force which surrounds us everywhere? Energy performs miracles and is capable of representing itself in countless ways. Science tries to make logic of energy for our own understanding yet on the most primitive level it seems energy is a manifested collective conscious. For mankind to move forward energy must be understood beyond any point of implied science. By connecting energy to our emotional state of being we just might be able to move beyond our current realm. Above all, what is learned from understanding must be treated with responsible manor, attentiveness, and harmony.

My number is thirteen,
I am one surrounded by twelve.

Everyone on Earth is connected with each other, the planet, and the universe by a gentle form of energy resonating deeply beyond our wildest imagination. Life is an awesome gift and a calling for us to share unconditionally without hesitation. Everything we know changes life for the better when it's pure and true with honest intent.

We are the students,
The universe is our teacher.

Humans are the only known living beings on Earth who demonstrate an unmatched level of intelligence capable of building automation, saving lives, and questioning existence. It's not unreasonable to believe the human population is a product of alien seeding or alien experiments, *no other animal on this planet opens each other up with tools to save a life!* Instead they move on and focus on their own survival.

Alien abduction victims and third-kind encounter witnesses often bring daunting recollections to the table that even twists the heads of respected psychologists. There is no monetary gain; In fact many victims feel humiliated by mass-media's attempts to convince the general public that anything to do with aliens is likely a hoax. Part of mass-media's problem is the restrictive nature of operations through a steady distribution of controlled information. Governments seek to prevent mass hysteria like that resulting from Orson Welles 1938 radio drama about an alien invasion, War of the Worlds, instilling panic among the public during the height of war.

At the moment, alien existence cannot be proven or disproved although a growing body of logical evidence is swaying to the fact their existence is more likely than not. Mathematics can even put estimated numbers to it using formulas such as the Drake Equation to estimate probability of life on other planets in the universe. One of the more astounding aspects found in reports of alien visitations, the testing and experiments aliens are performing are nearly identical to experiments humans perform on animals.

It may seem probable that life exists elsewhere in the universe, but many believe it's less likely Earth would be visited by it. Examining light from distant stars and planets will only tell us so much. The window for communicating with alien life millions of light years away is incredibly narrow, entire civilizations on distant planets could go extinct in the blink of an eye due to the time factor alone. However, if mankind created a method of interstellar travel, or communication, we might be able to overcome odds of life's adversities once again, this time on a monumental scale.

Our ancient ancestors believed their ancestors descended from the sky, or ascended from the Earth in some cultures, for reasons beyond current explanation. They worked hard to preserve oral traditions of creation to the point of carving history into stone while determining our place in the cosmos.

Perhaps people have been tucked away on the lush planet Earth for protection, as a *contingency plan*, in the preservation of our species. Aliens are assumed to be creatures of a different kind as seemingly fitting to the diversity of life on our planet, but what if aliens are actually human? It's an interesting thought to consider, that our ancient relatives were responsible for the destruction of dinosaurs via asteroid bombing, to clear the Earth's surface for us to live upon.

For the prosperity of mankind.

Mainstream religions state we were made in the image of god, the image part is not limited to appearance only. If we are a carbon copy, a reproduction, or a representation, then might that also include our thoughts, intelligence, subconscious, and behavior? In this case, our actions on Earth would mimic those of our creators and thus explain why we are the way we are, such as creating seed storage banks to preserve the life of Earth in the chance of a global catastrophe.

Imagine what an epic impact this would have if mankind discovered not only that we're not alone, but also that aliens are actually humans living in the distant reaches of the universe, who seeded Earth to ensure survival of the species outside of more dangerous areas. In the probability of quantum mechanics, this is one possible outcome. Until such a time redefines our very existence we must continue to push forward to discover new concepts about the universe.

We can overcome an artificial structure of a corrupt world economy, we can stop senseless fighting amongst ourselves like needy children in a sandbox, we can put aside our differences and band together in peace. Together we will accomplish anything imaginable and literally rise above to explore the great expanse of our universe. We will discover who we really are, and finally solidify our place in the cosmos. Of course, all we have to do is *put our minds to it*.

J.C. Vintner